Rock'n'Rollin' ENCORE BOOK

ABOUT THE BOOK

The Rock'n'Rollin' series is a drum set curriculum designed for kids to learn the instruments of a drum set and to read and play drum music as as young as 5 years old. Rock'n'Rollin' Encore is an extension of the Level 1 Method that includes 20 more on-staff solos students can play and 18 more activities students can complete during their lessons or for homework.

USING THE BOOK

Rock'n'Rollin' Encore Level 1 uses the simplified staff found in unit 6 of Rock'n'Rollin' Level 1. You can use the book in tandem with or as an extension of the Level 1 book before moving to Level 2.

ABOUT ZACH SECKMAN

Zach Seckman is an active Musician, Studio Teacher, Music Director, and Composer/Arranger living in Wichita, KS. Seckman is the owner of Seckman Music Studio where he teaches drums, ukulele, piano and voice lessons. Aside from Rock'N'Rollin', Zach has also created the *Little Jammers Kids Band* curriculum which teaches Guitar, Drums, Vocals, and Keyboards in a band format to ages 4-7. In his lack-of spare time, Zach enjoys reading, cooking, and playing Super Nintendo.

What's In This Book?

THIS BOOK BELONGS TO:

Student: ________________________________ Phone: _______________

Teacher: ________________________________ Phone: _______________

____

All The Instruments

Remember all these instruments on the drum set? And do you remember where they live on the staff??

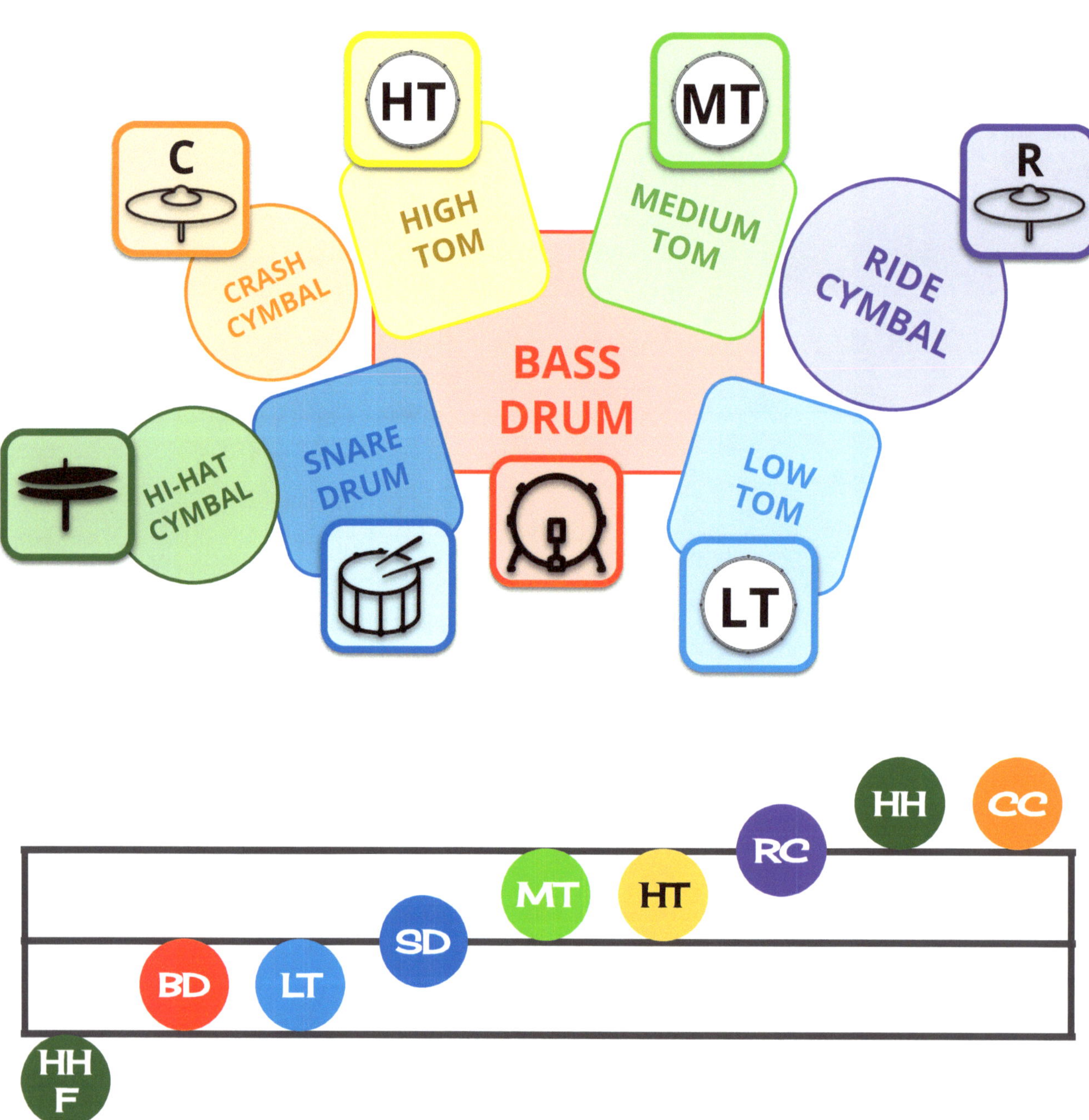

Ready to Run

Double check and see what instruments you play before starting.

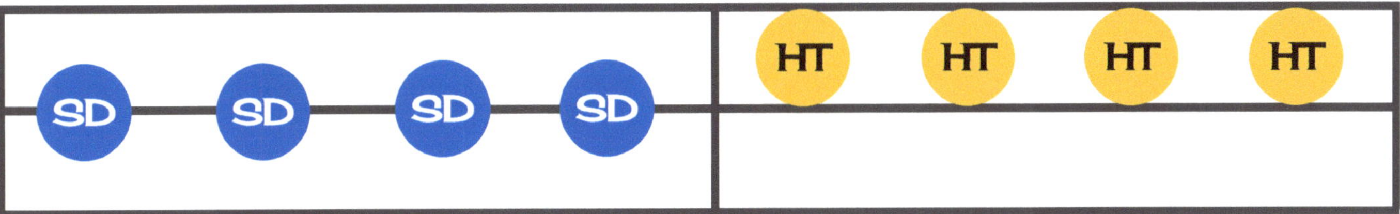

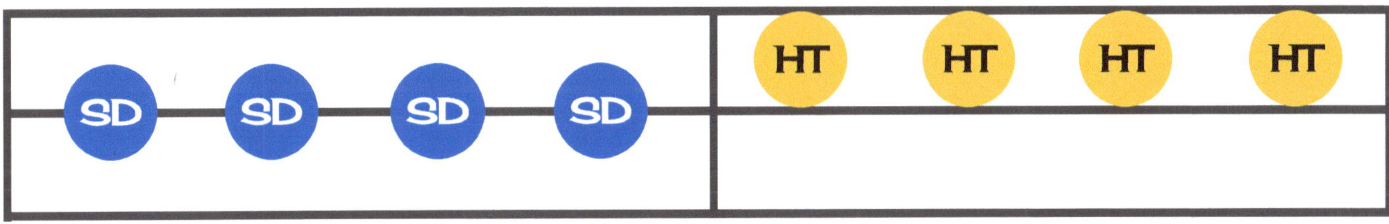

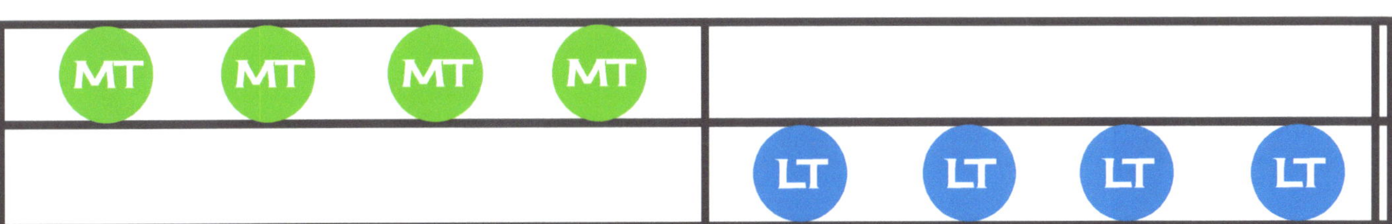

Totally Toms

Remember what the black X at the end of the song means?

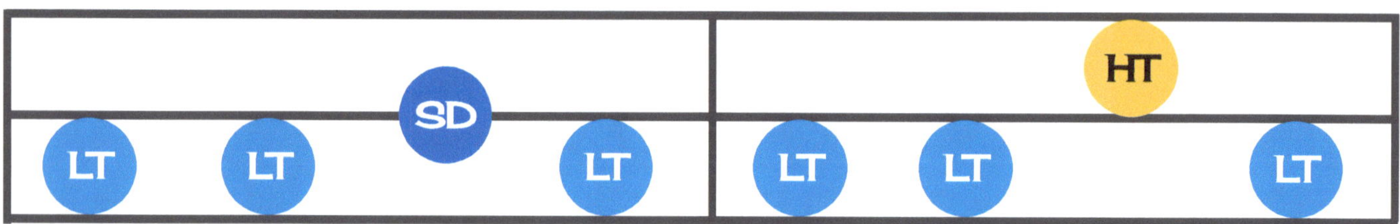

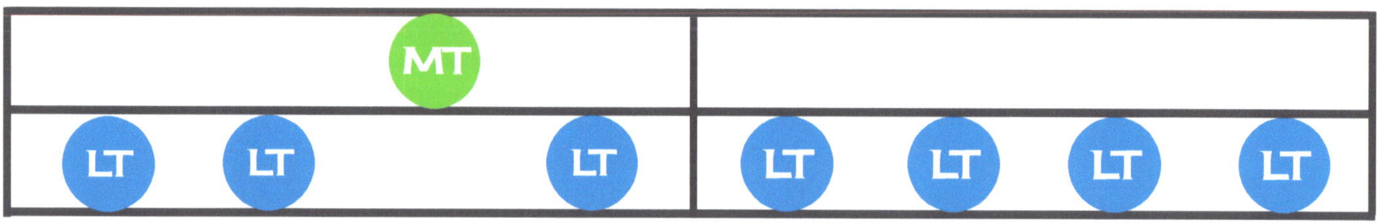

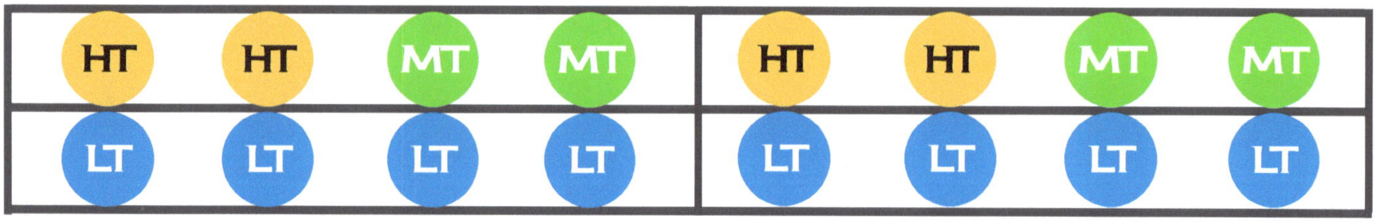

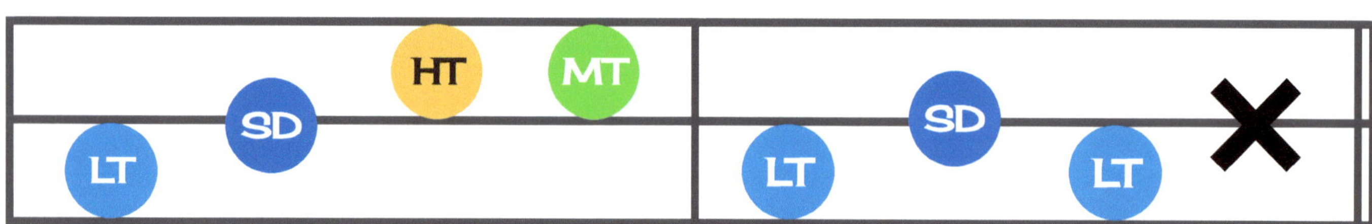

Back and Forth

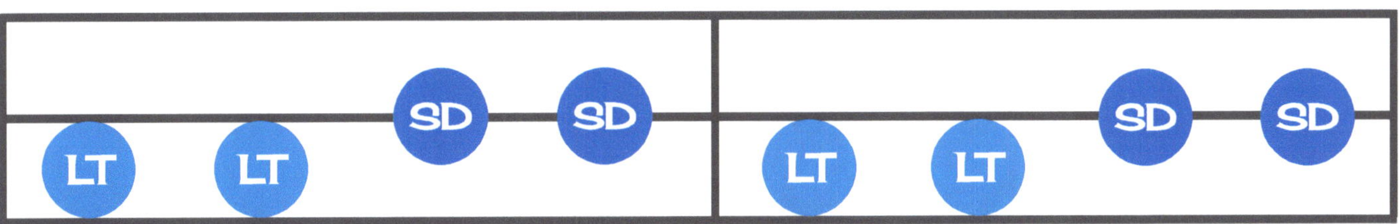

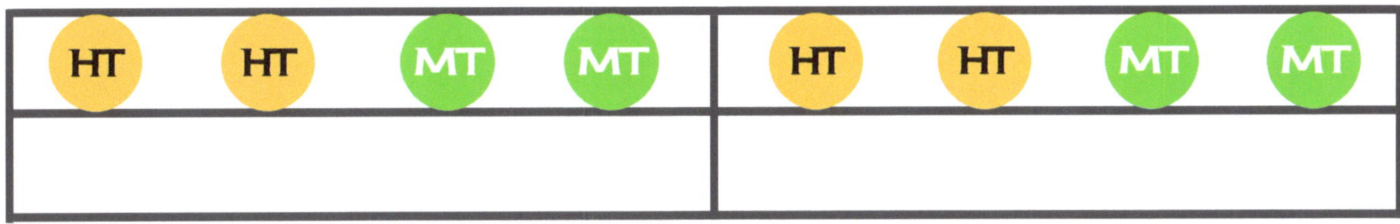

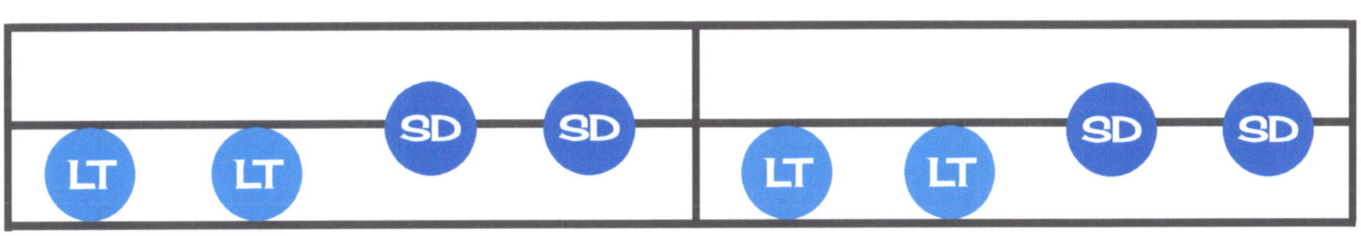

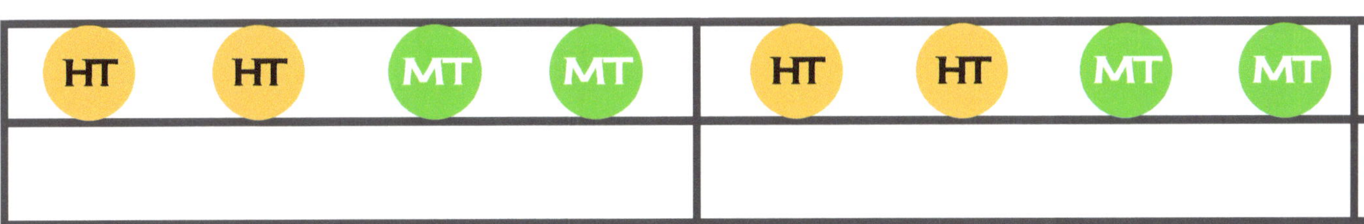

Bottoms Up!

BD BD BD BD LT LT LT LT

SD SD SD SD MT MT HT HT

BD BD BD BD LT LT LT LT

SD SD SD SD MT MT HT HT

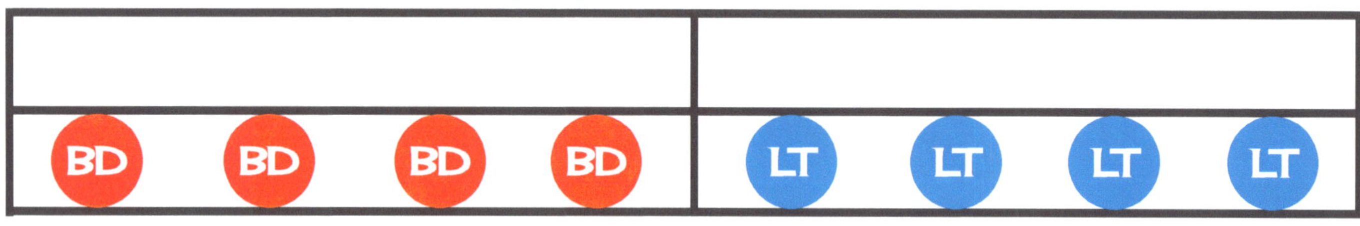

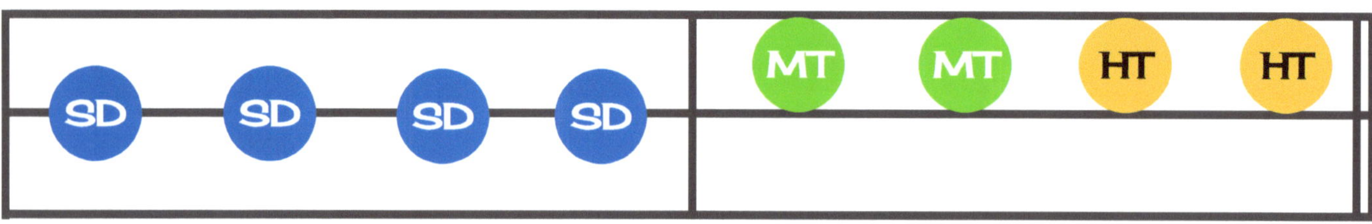

Times Two

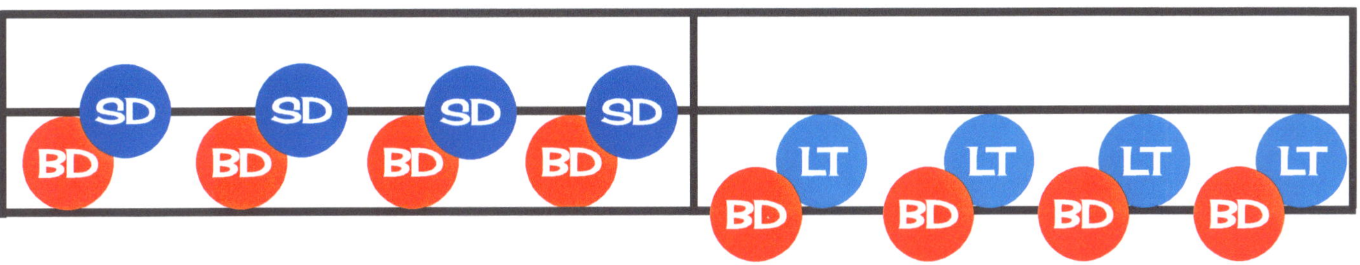

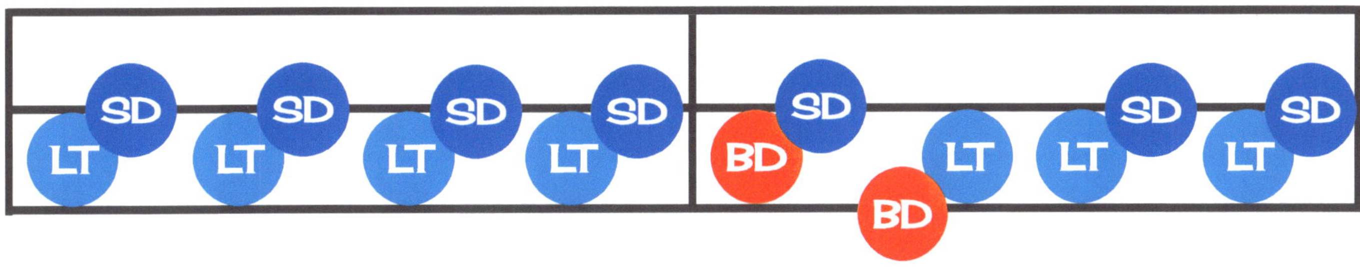

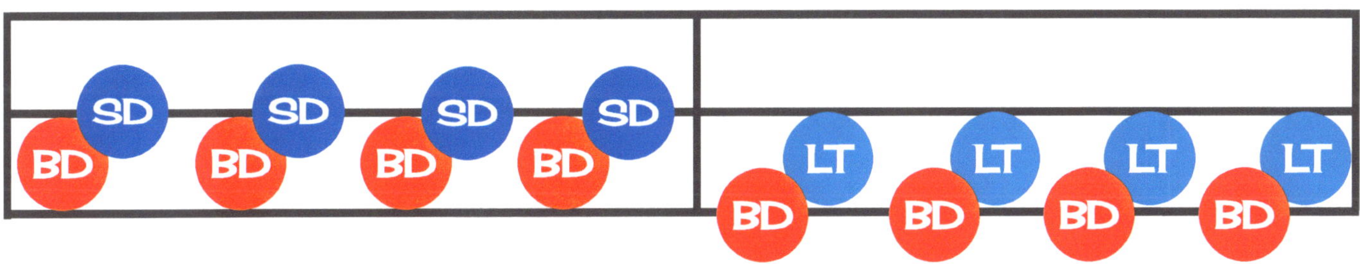

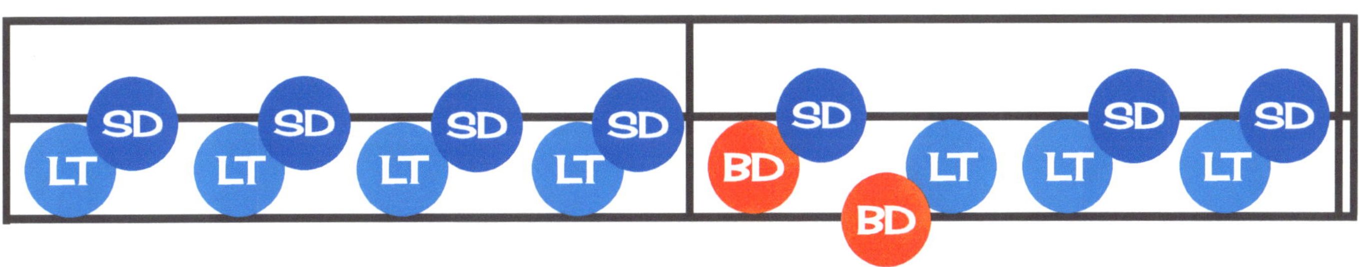

Simple on the Staff

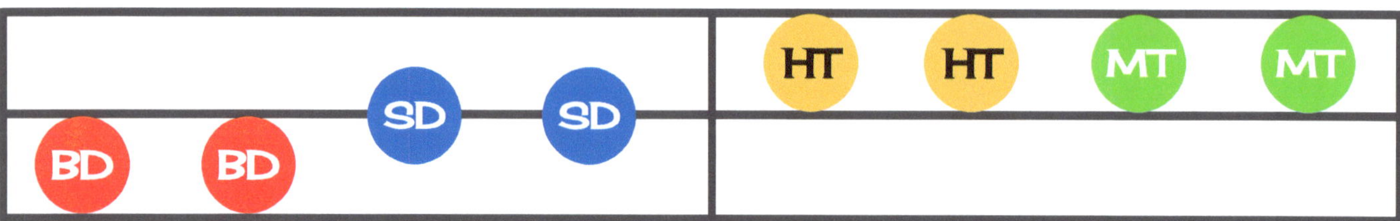

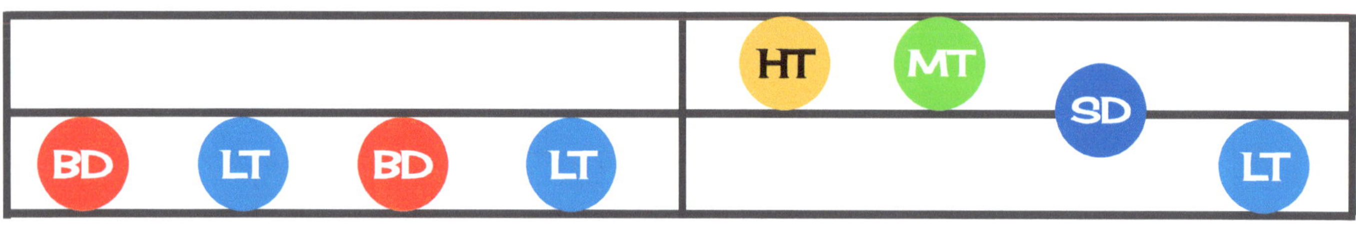

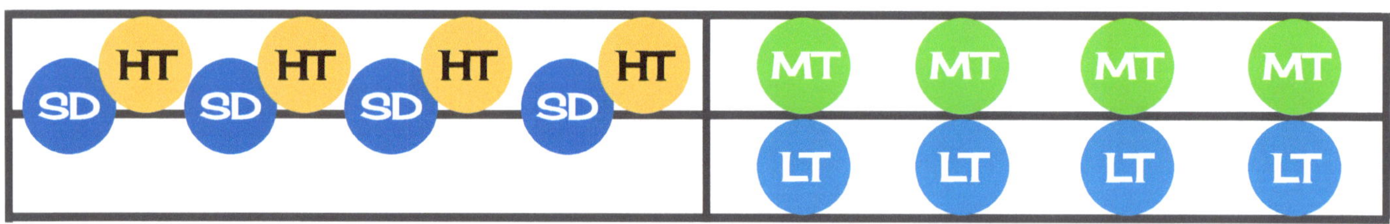

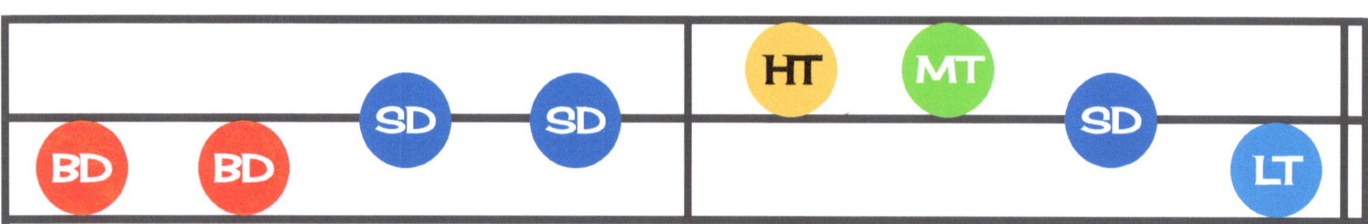

1-Beat Stomp

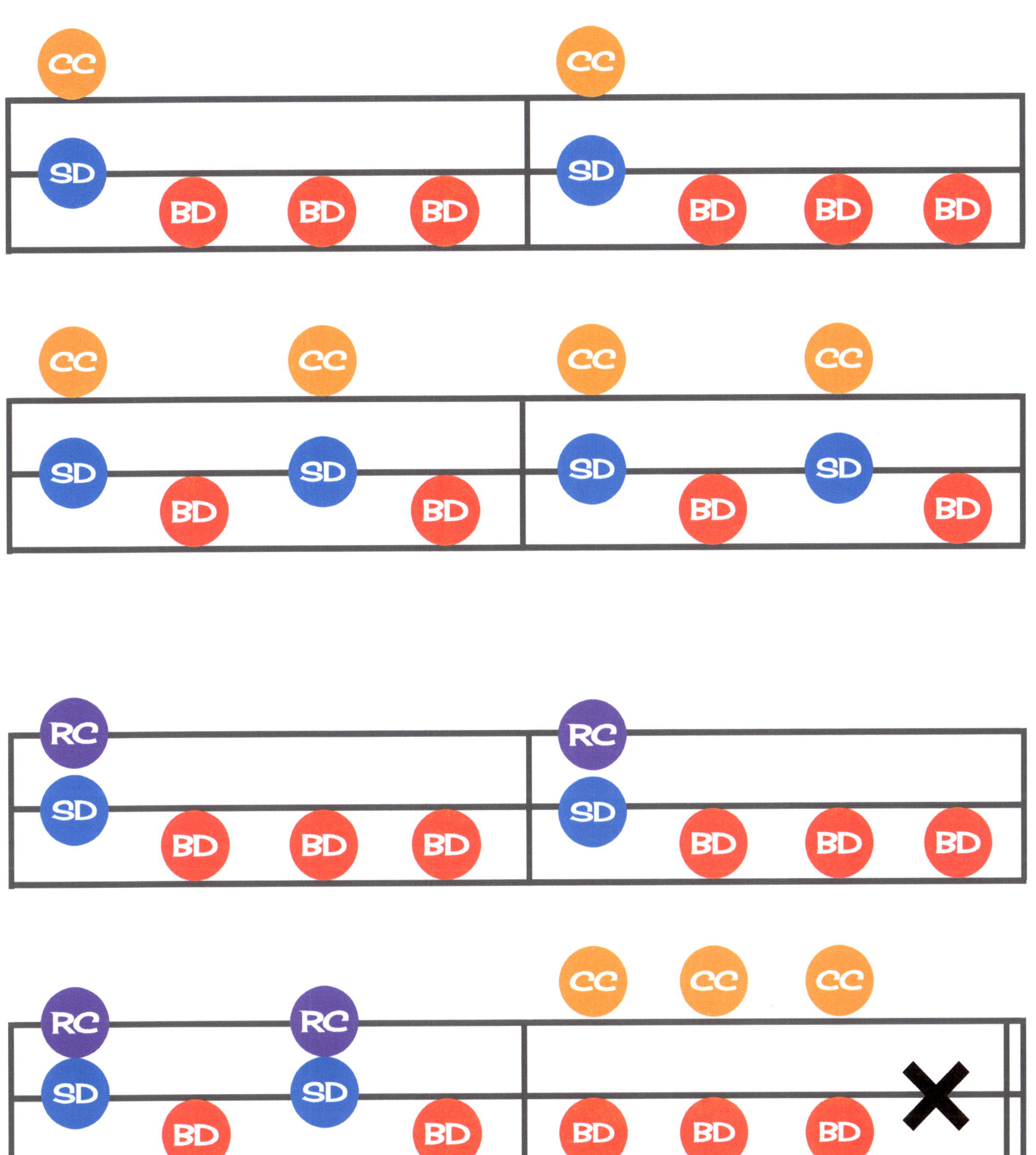

2-Beat Stomp

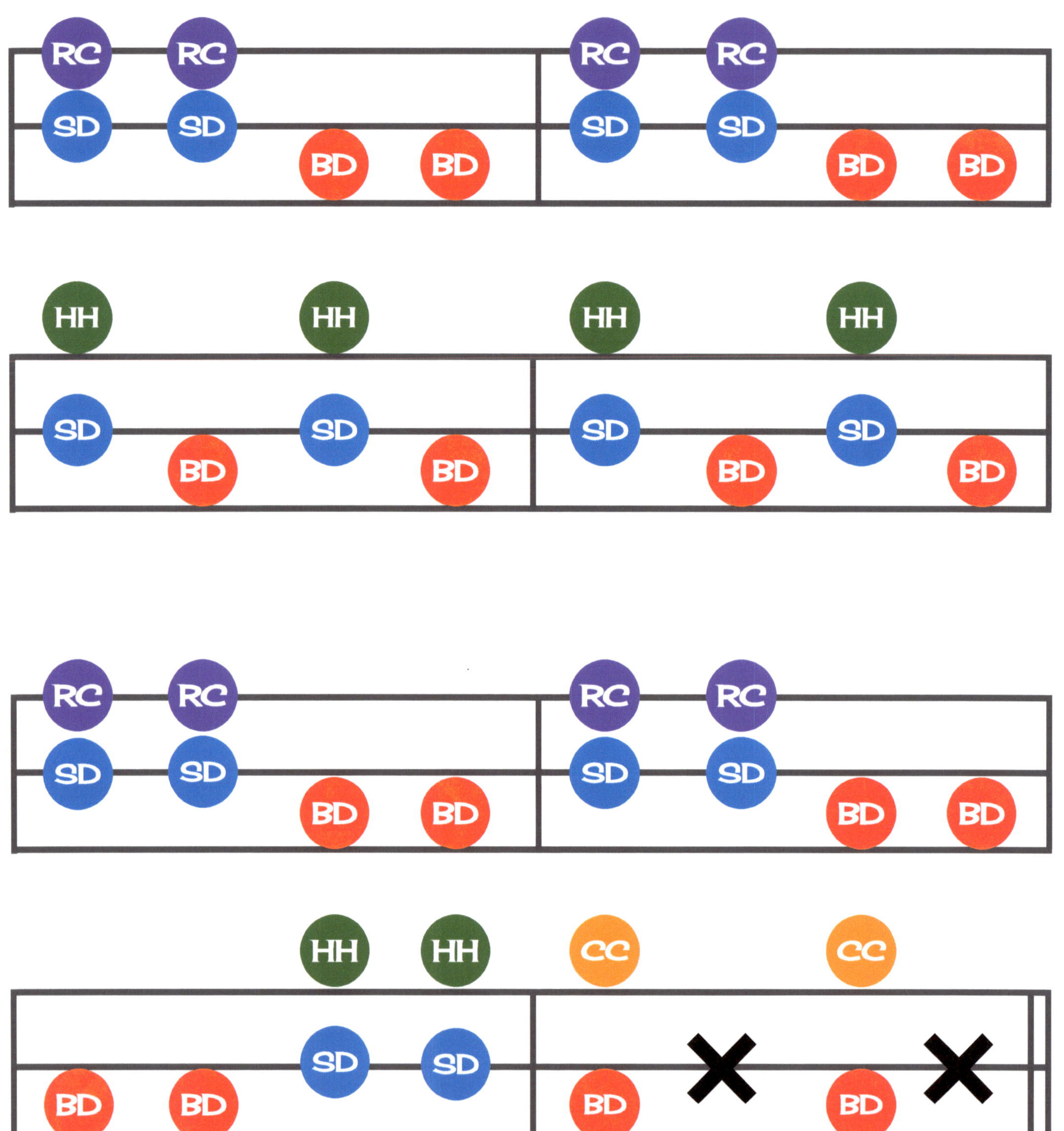

3-Beat Stomp

RC RC RC RC RC RC
SD SD SD SD SD SD
BD BD
HH HH HH HH HH HH
SD SD SD SD SD SD
BD BD
RC RC RC RC RC RC
SD SD SD SD SD SD
BD BD
HH HH HH HH HH HH HH CC
SD SD SD SD SD SD SD
BD

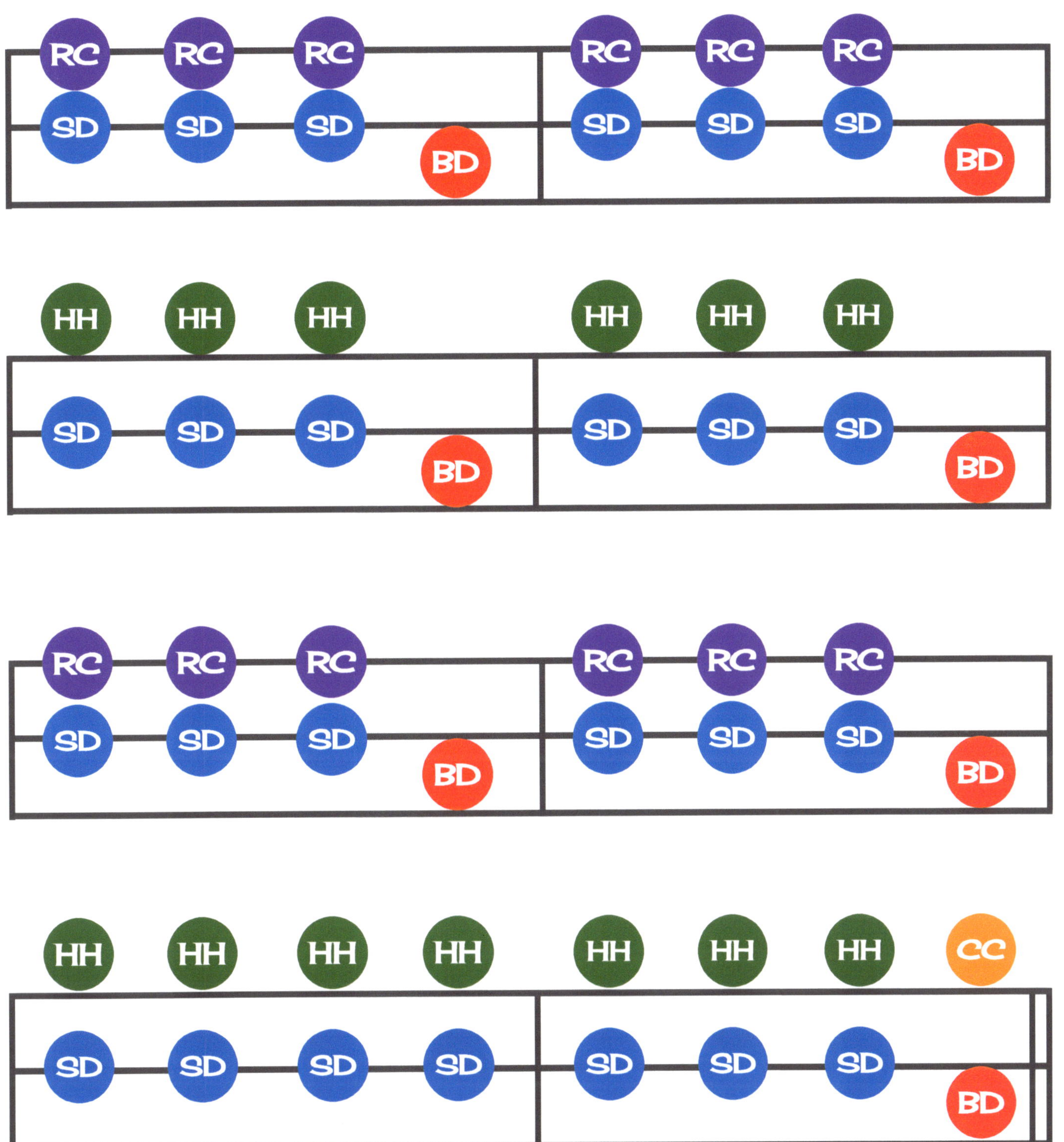

Basic Beat Bop

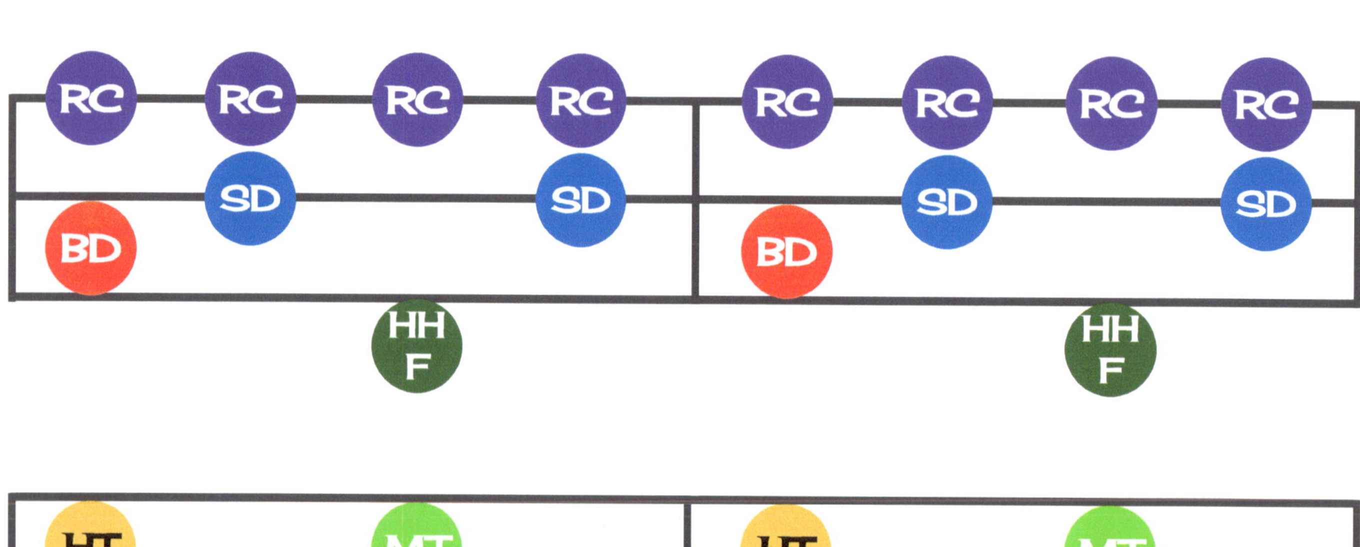

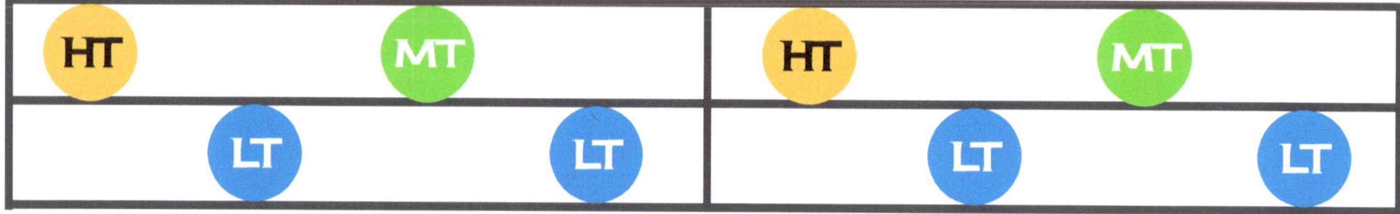

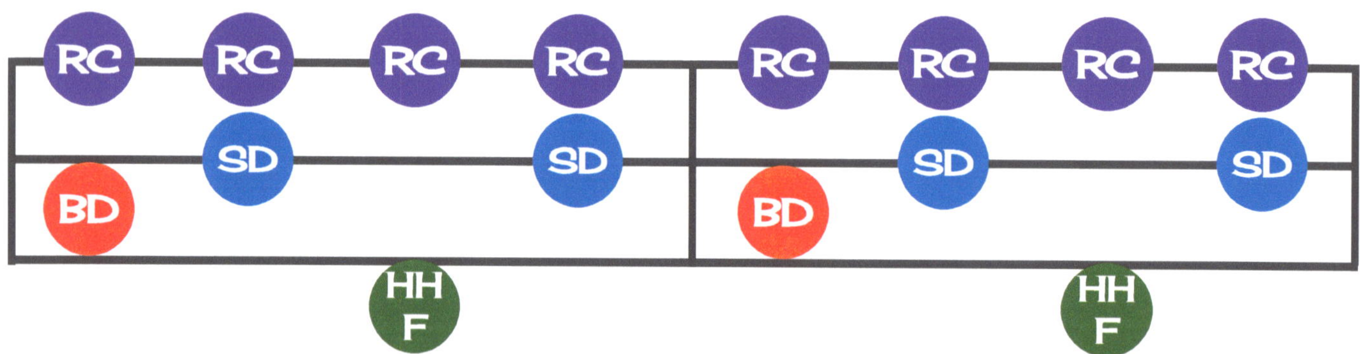

A High Crash Ride

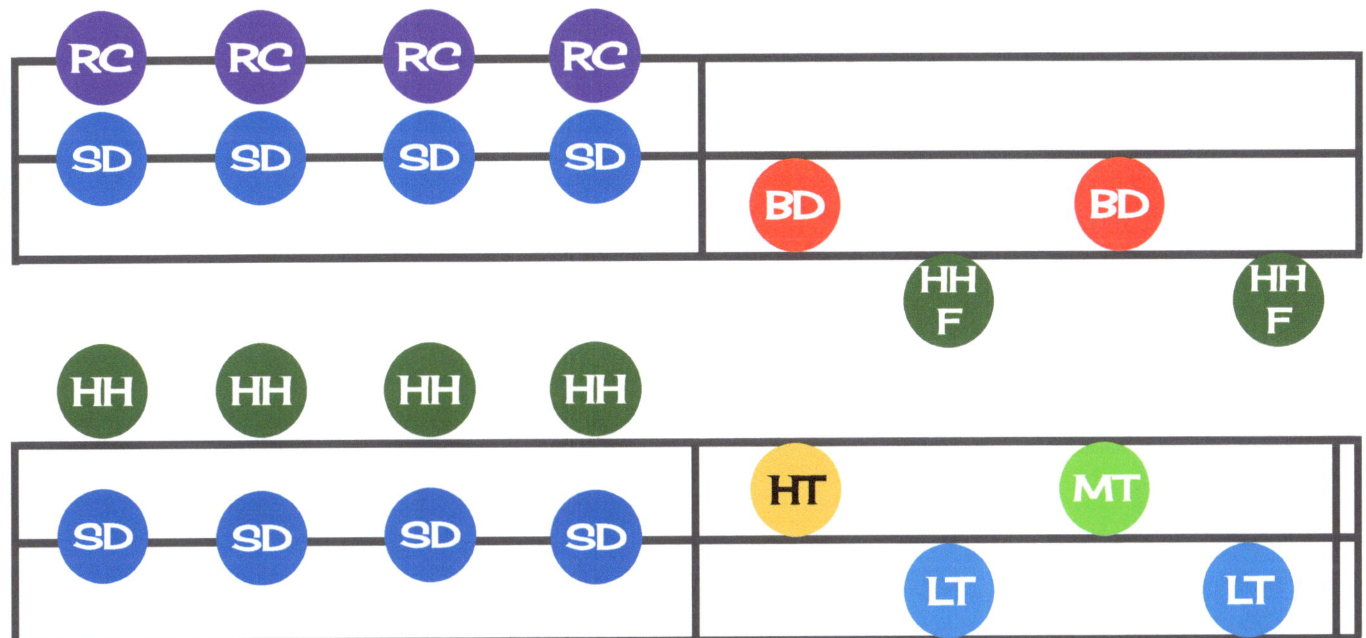

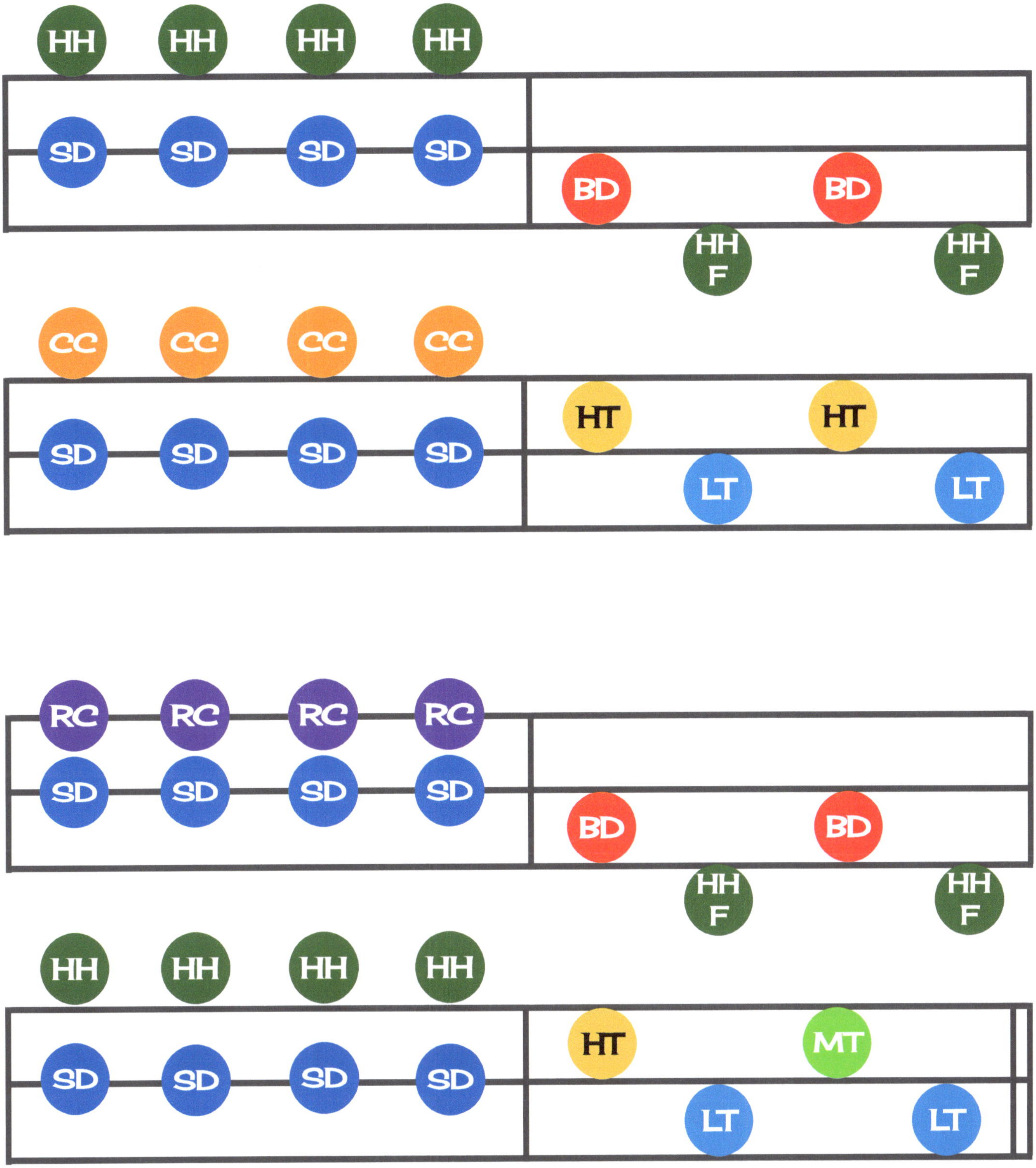

Going Up

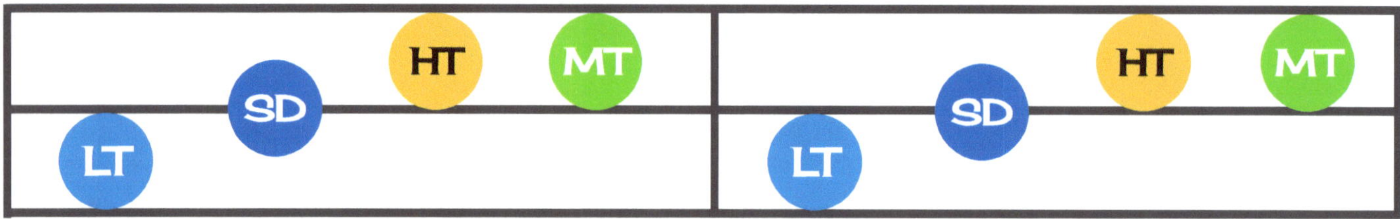

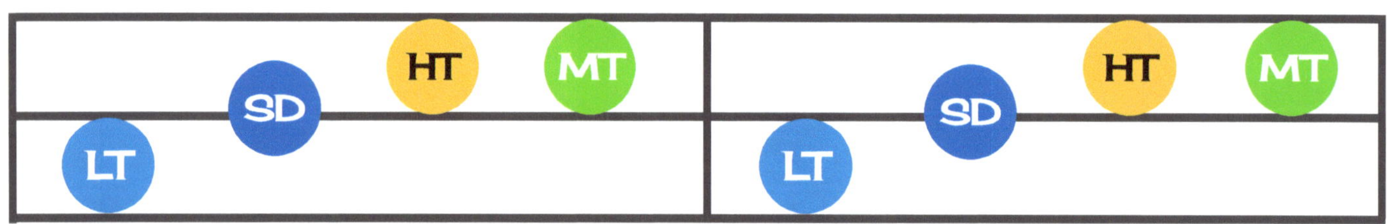

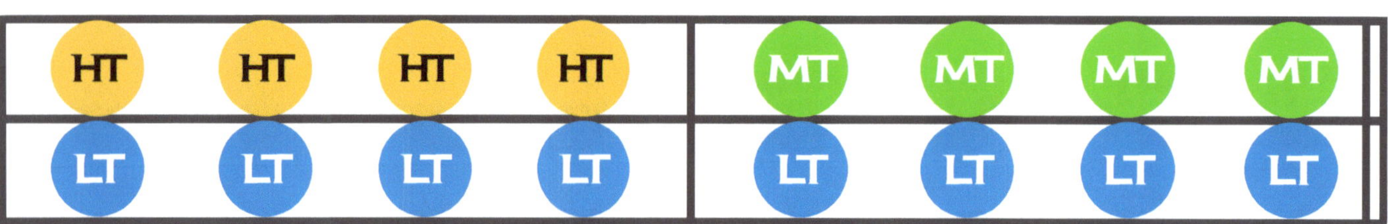

Riding to the Hats

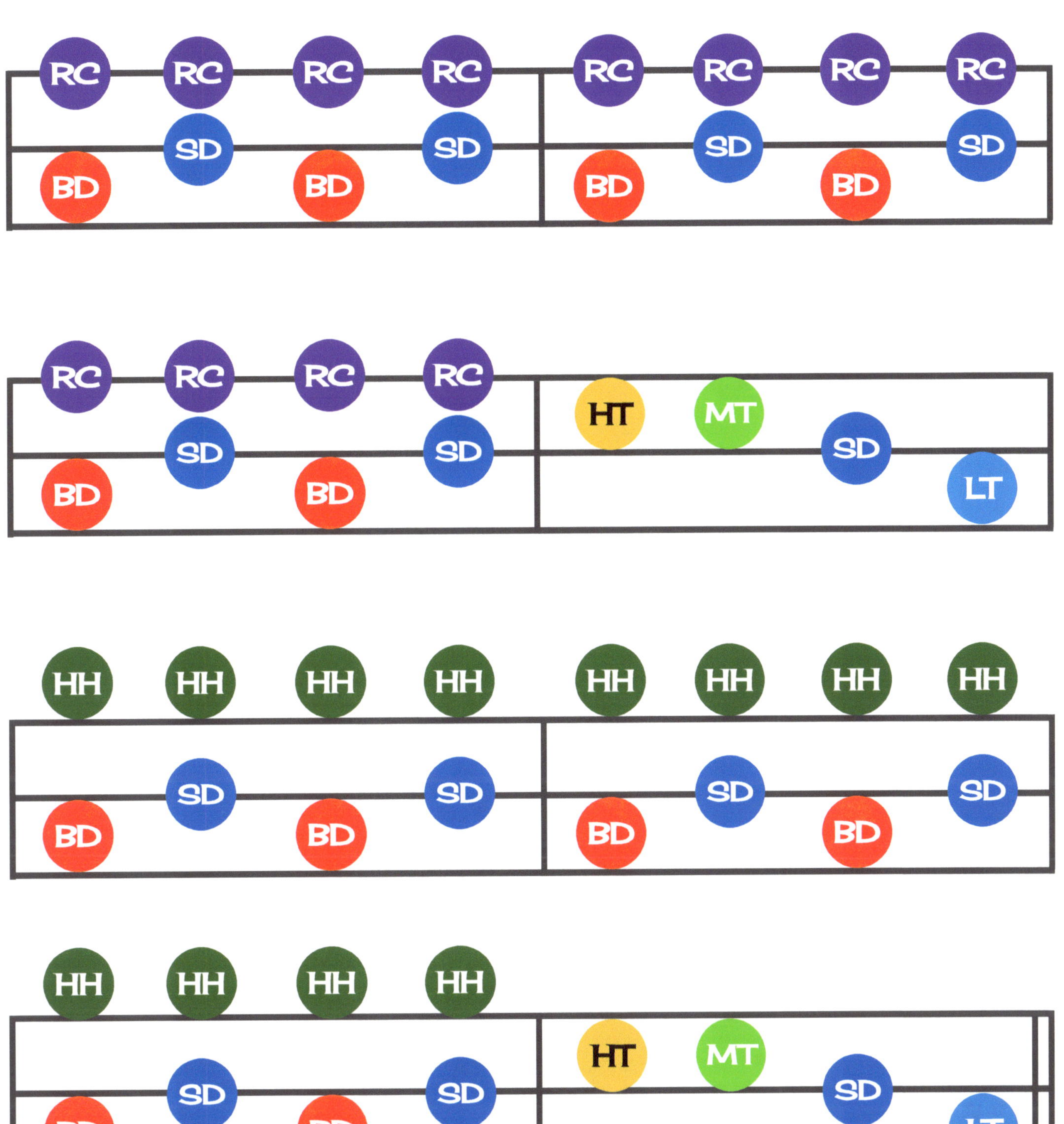

Play and Rest

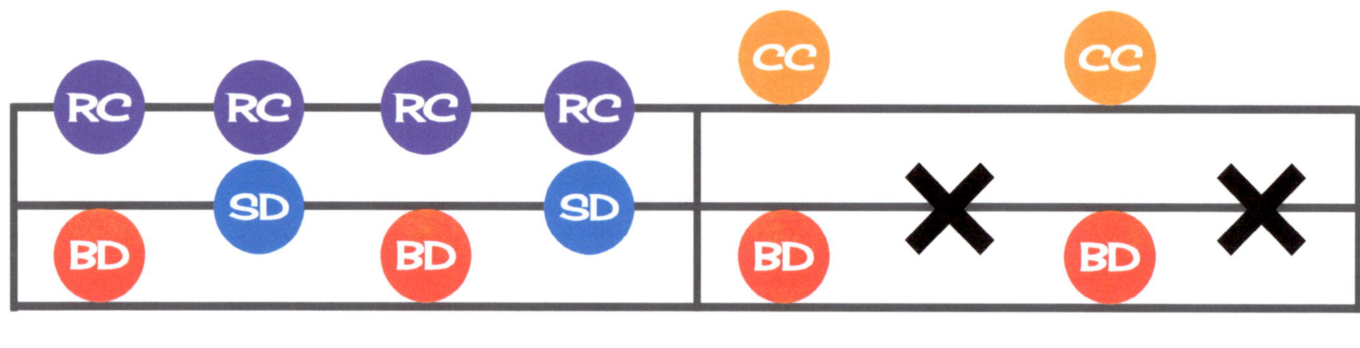

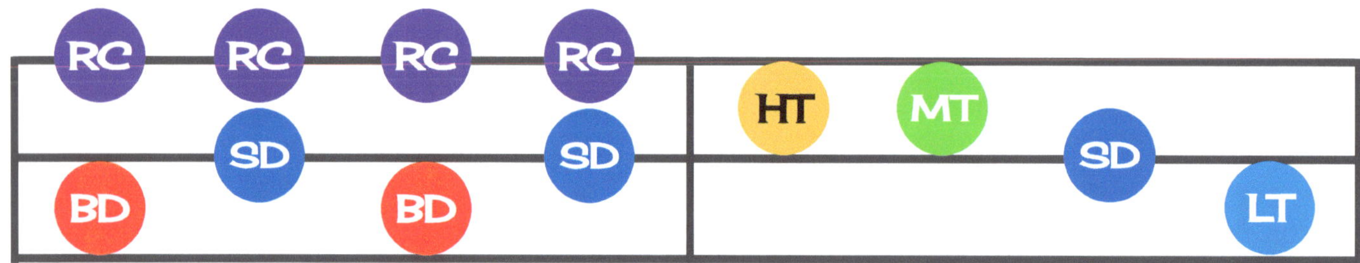

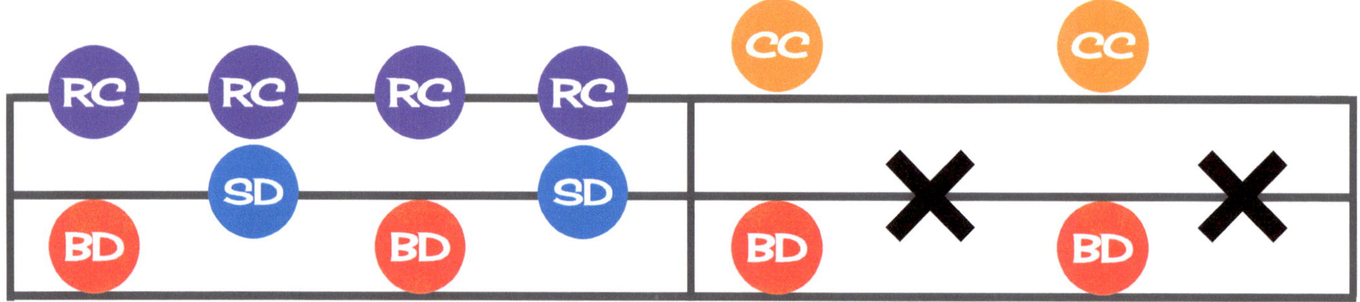

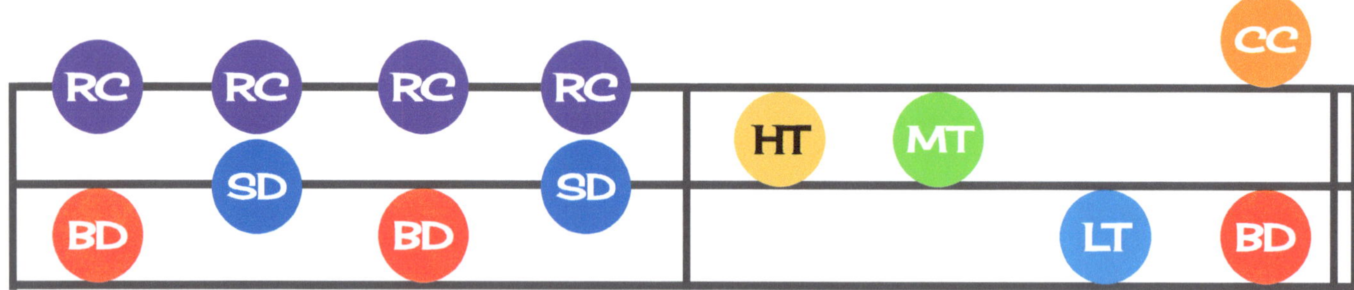

Snare Snap

RC RC RC RC RC RC RC RC
SD SD SD SD
BD BD
HH F HH F
SR SR SR SR SR HT MT LT
RC RC RC RC RC RC RC RC
SD SD SD SD
BD BD
HH F HH F
SR SR SR SR SR HT MT LT

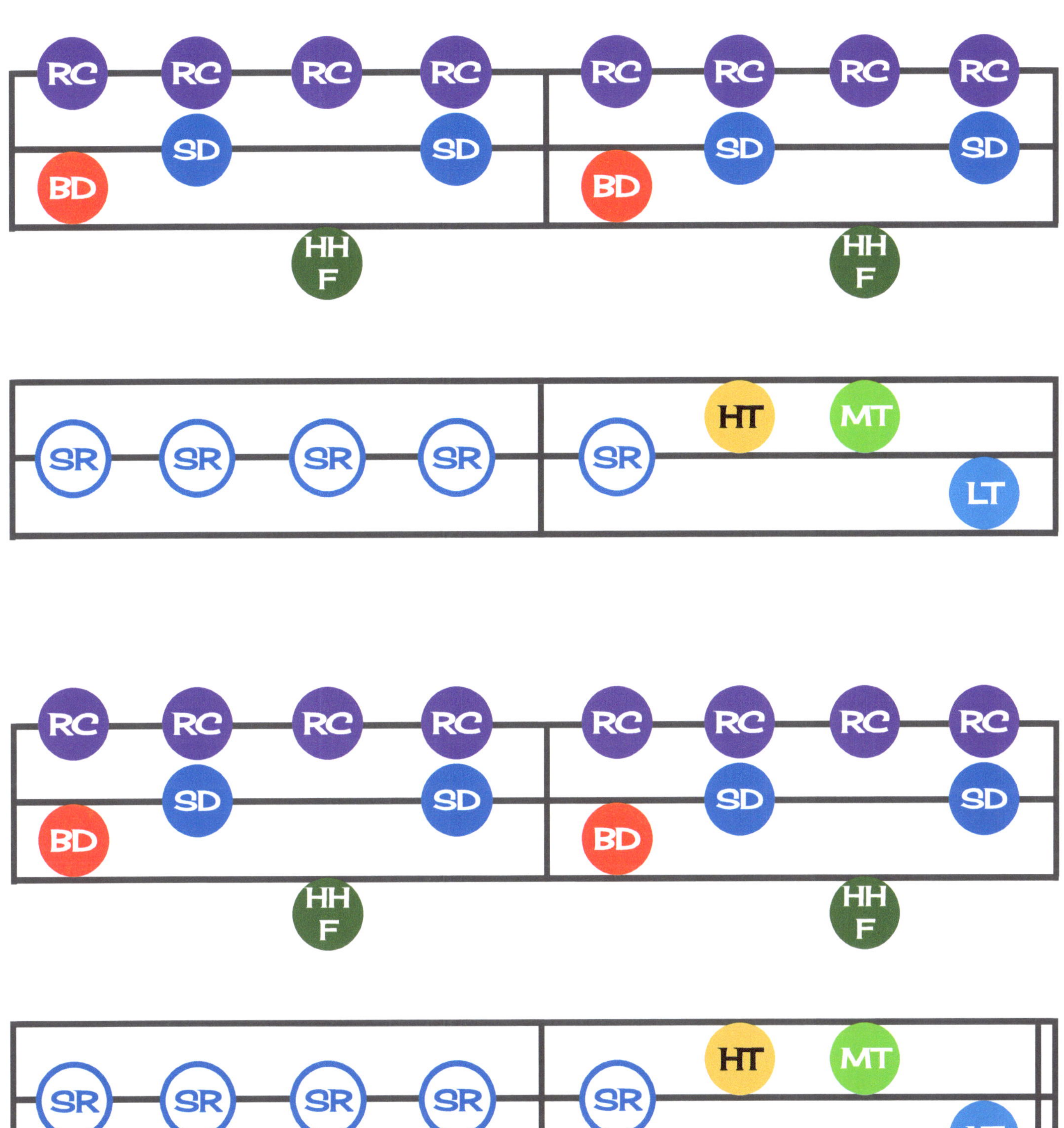

Bigger Beat Bop

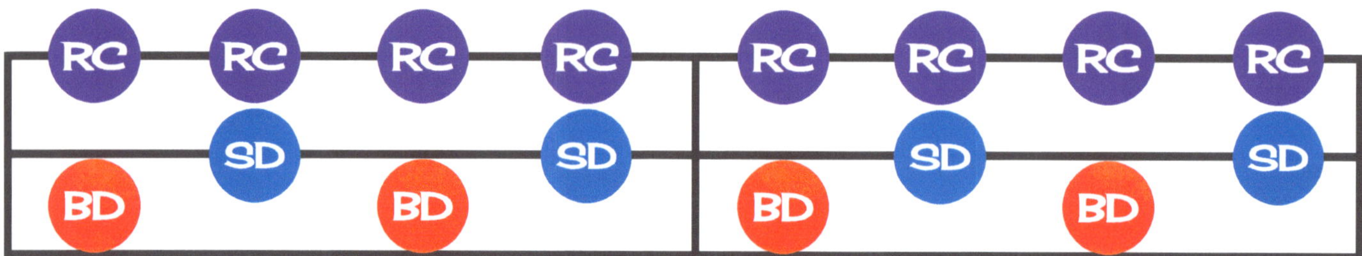

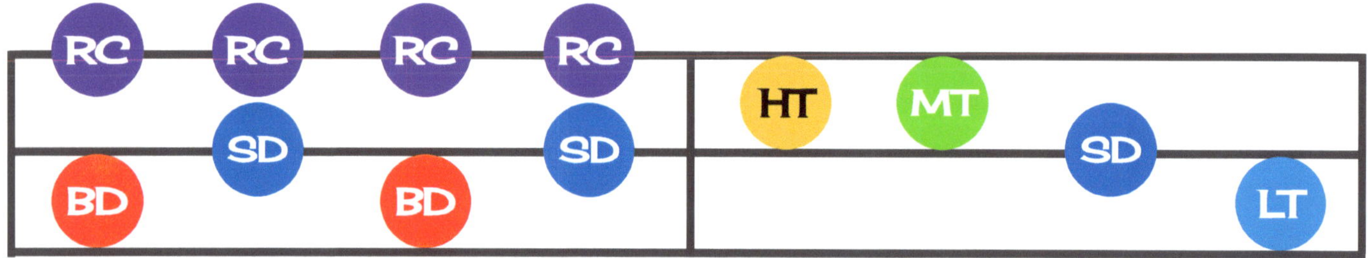

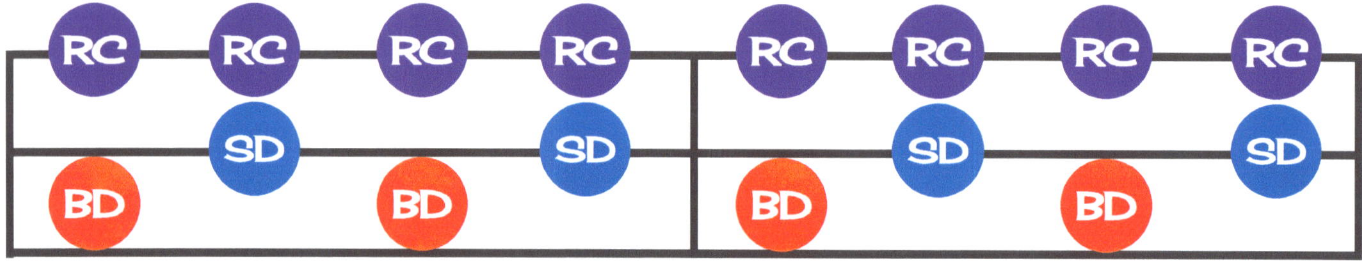

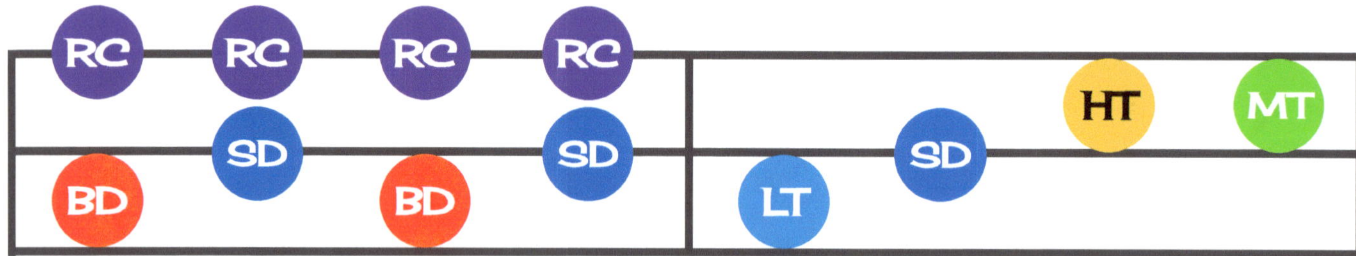

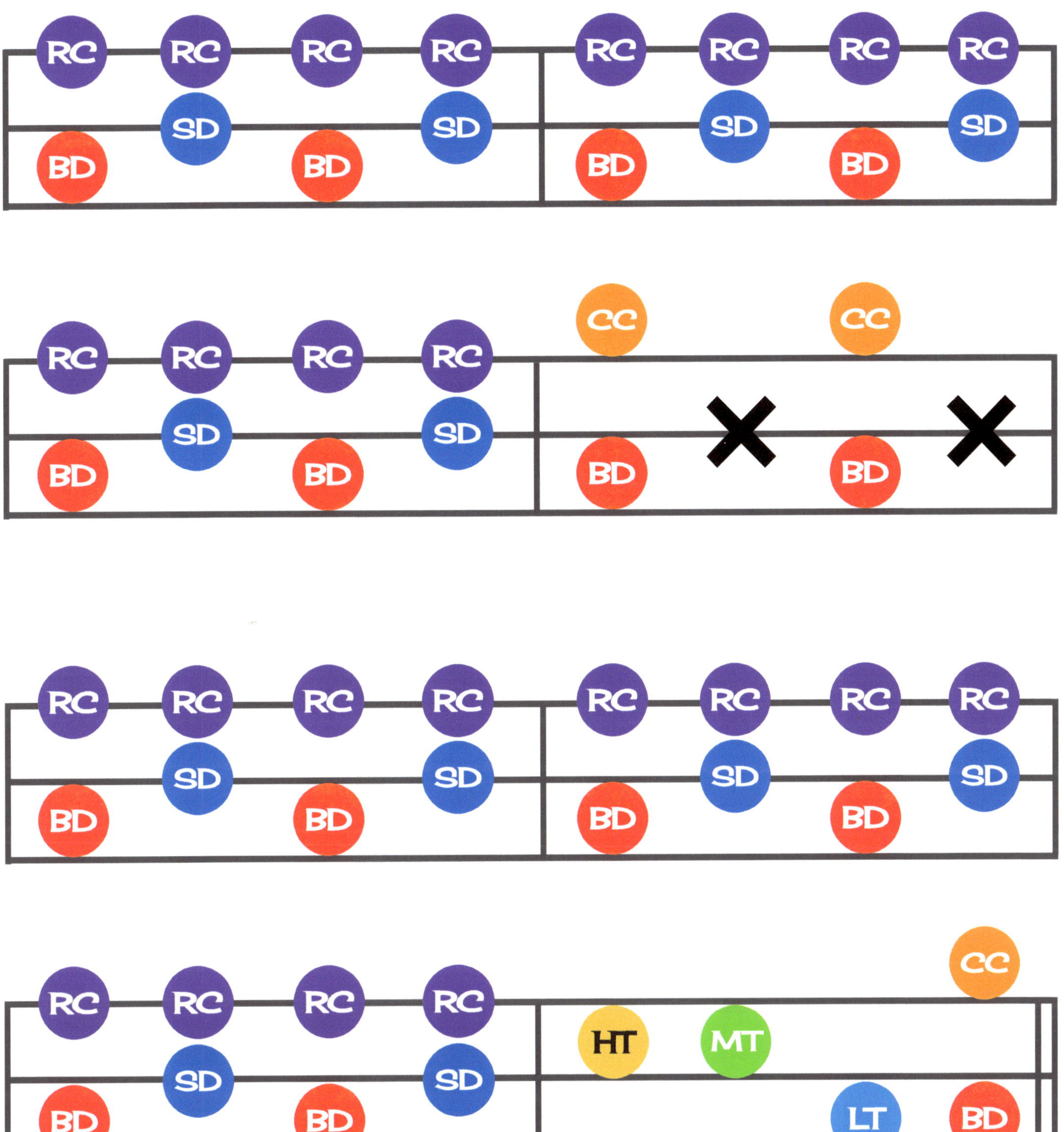

RC RC RC RC RC RC RC RC
SD SD SD SD
BD BD BD BD
RC RC RC RC CC CC
SD SD
BD X BD X
RC RC RC RC RC RC RC RC
SD SD SD SD
BD BD BD BD
RC RC RC RC CC
HT MT
SD SD
BD BD LT BD

Rest Three Times

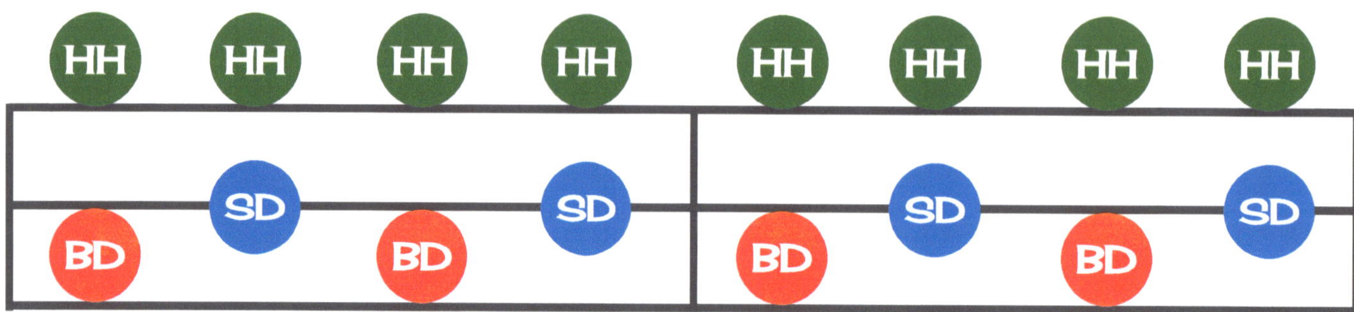

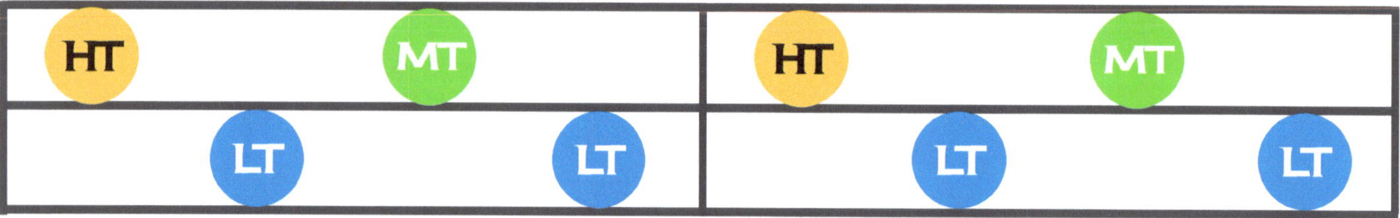

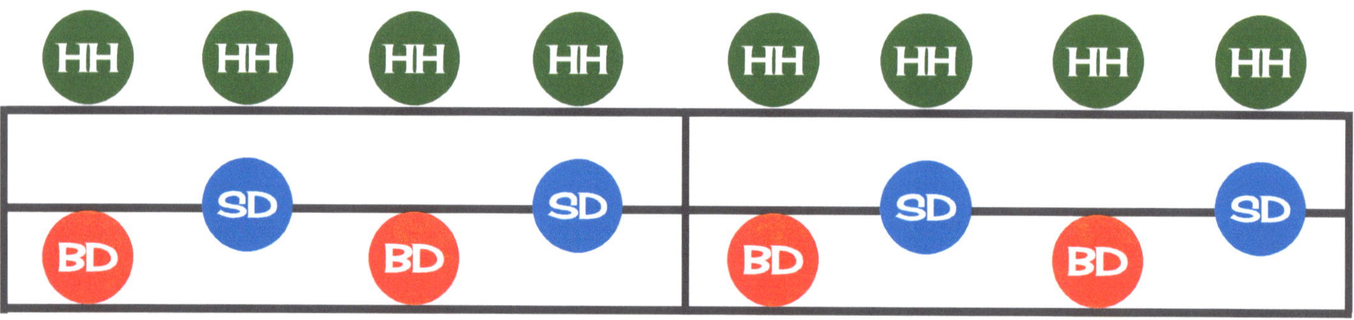

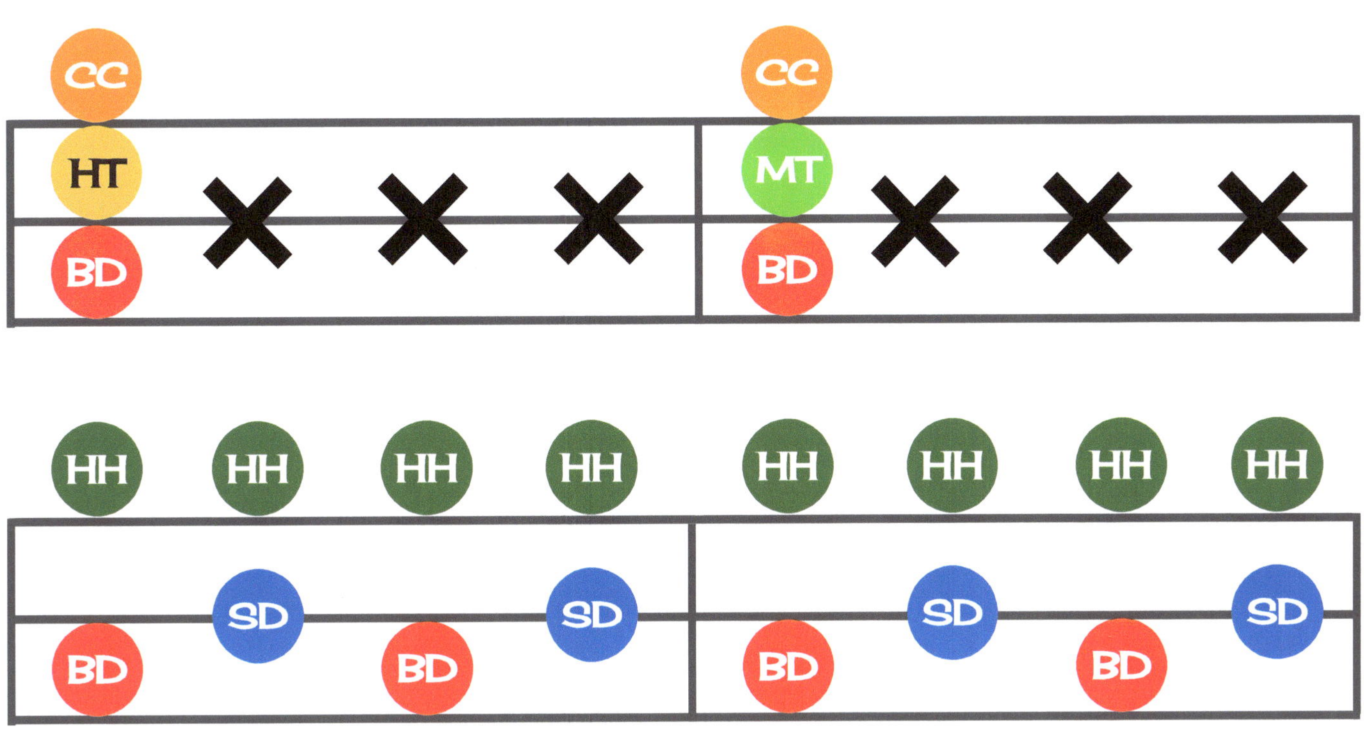
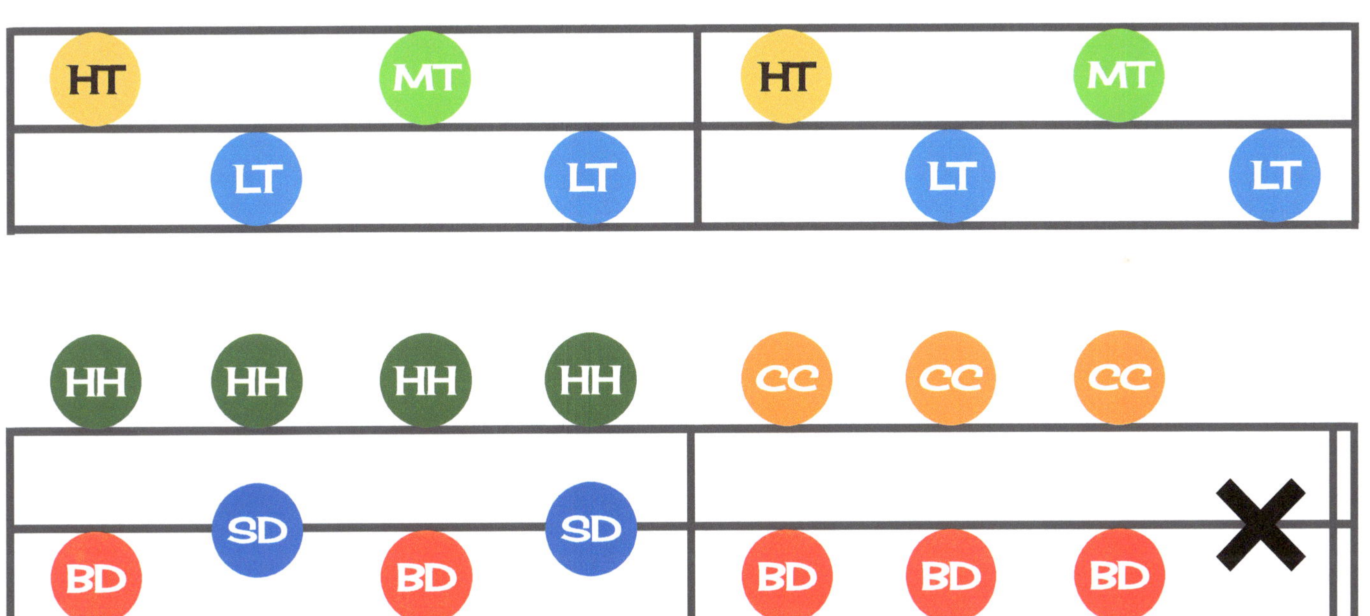

Building the Bass

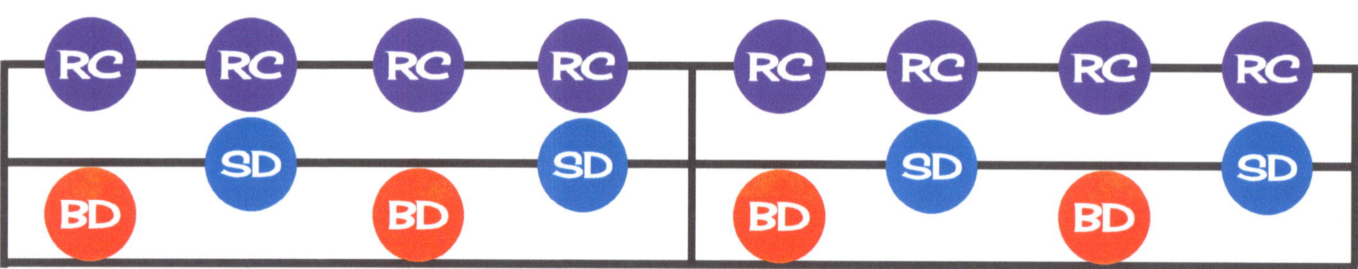

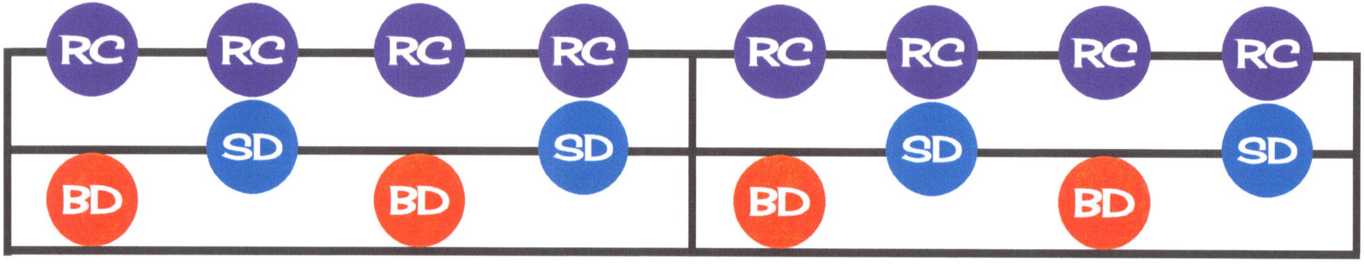

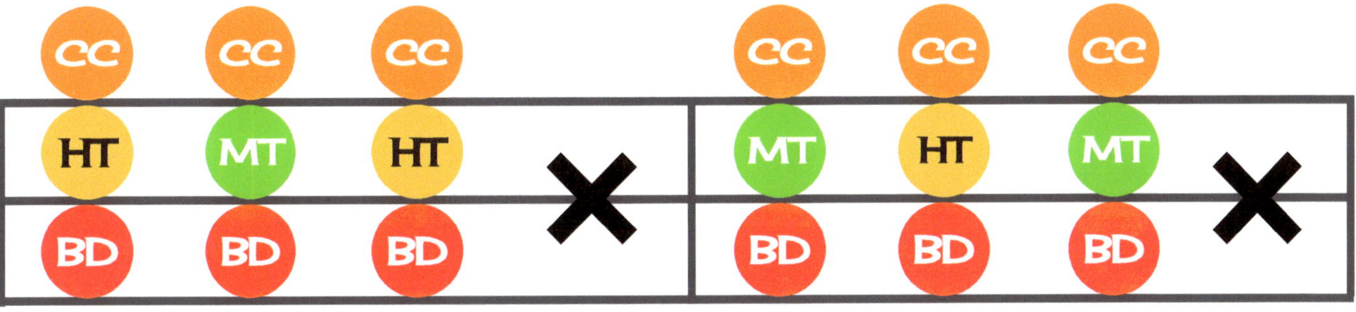
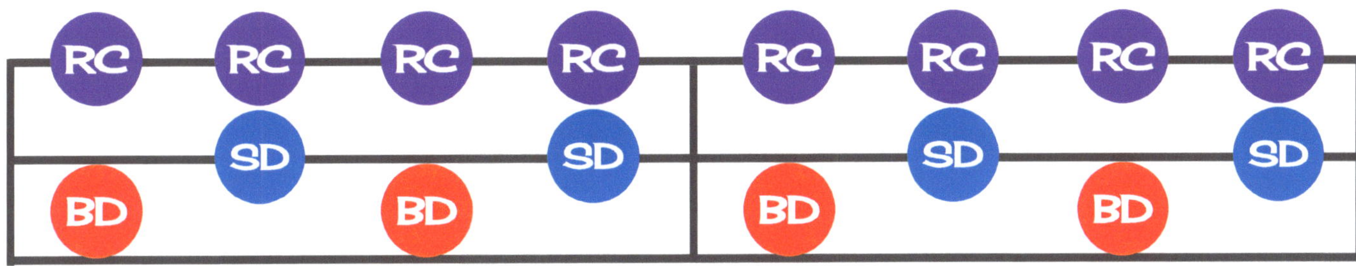
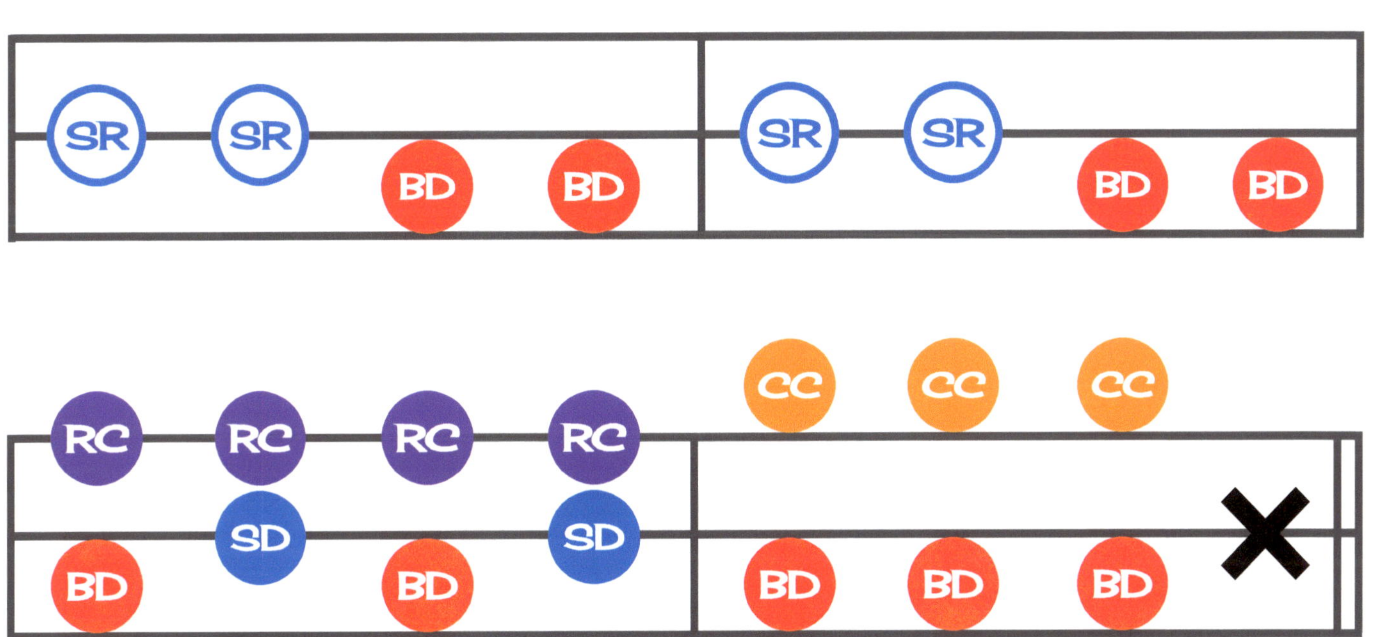

1-1-2

MT
HT
SD
LT
MT
HT
SD
LT

HT
MT
LT
BD
LT
BD
HT
MT
LT
LT
BD
BD

MT
HT
SD
LT
MT
HT
SD
LT

HT
MT
LT
BD
LT
BD
HT
MT
LT
LT
BD
BD

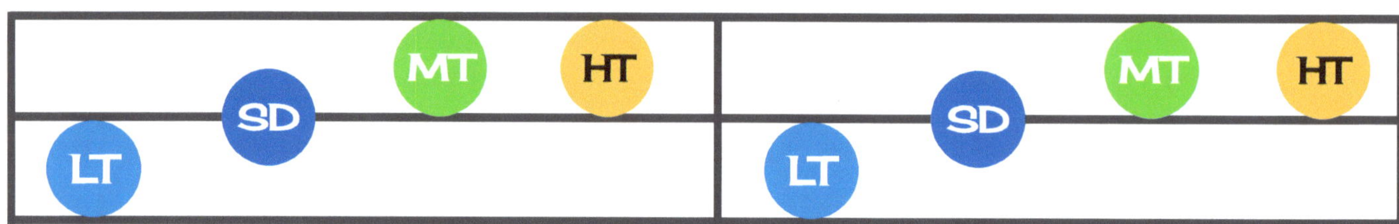

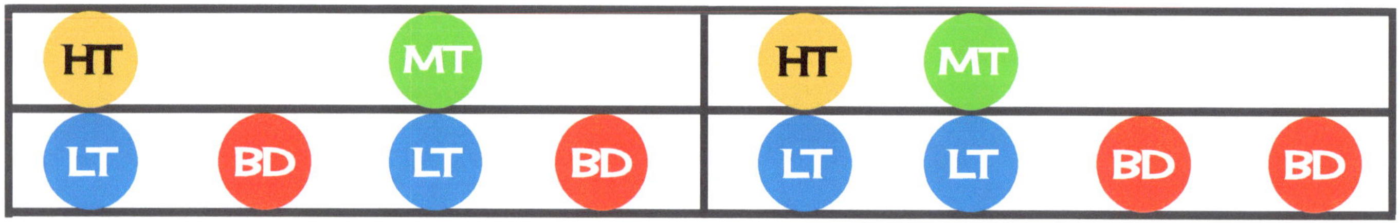

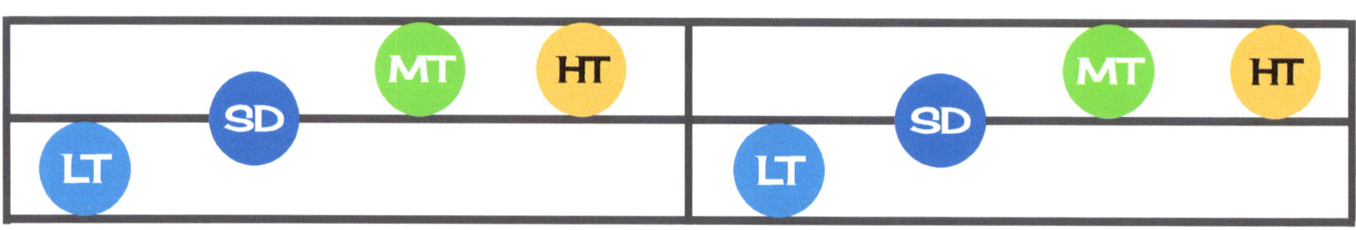

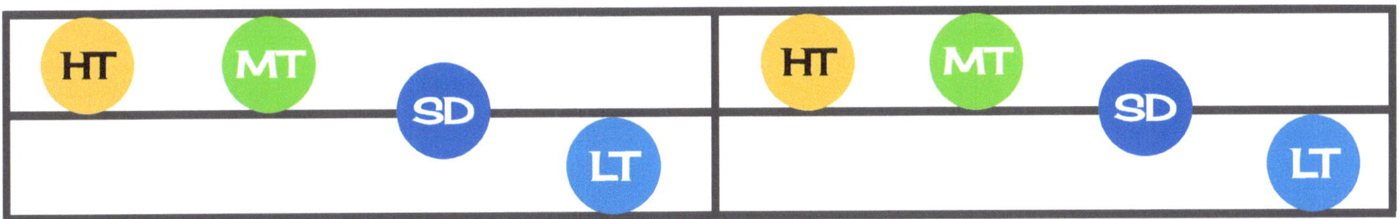

HT MT SD LT
HT MT SD LT

MT HT
LT BD LT BD
MT HT
LT LT BD BD

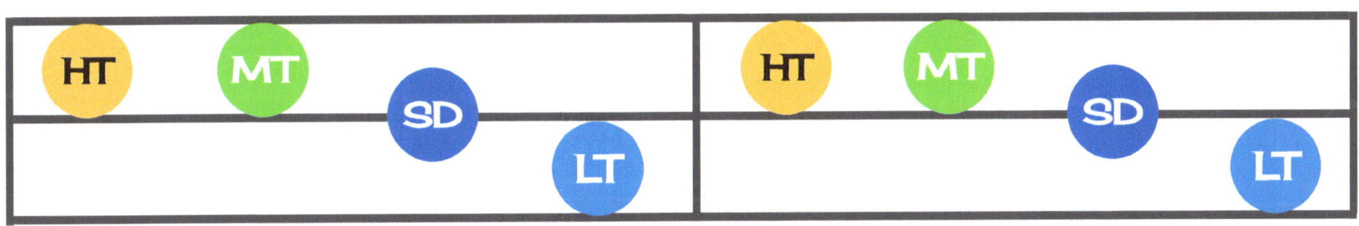

HT MT SD LT
HT MT SD LT

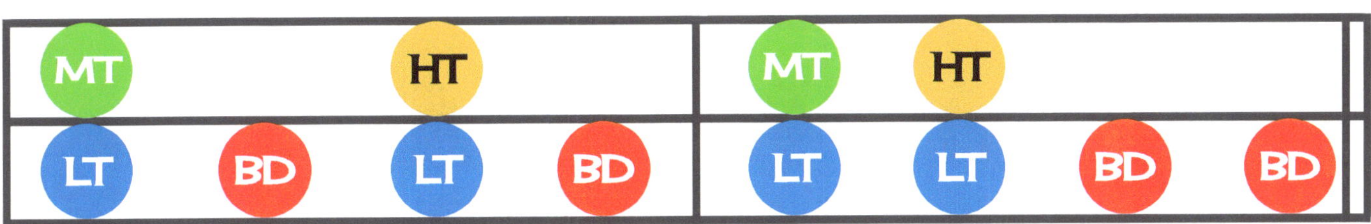

MT HT
LT BD LT BD
MT HT
LT LT BD BD

Low Tom Triumph

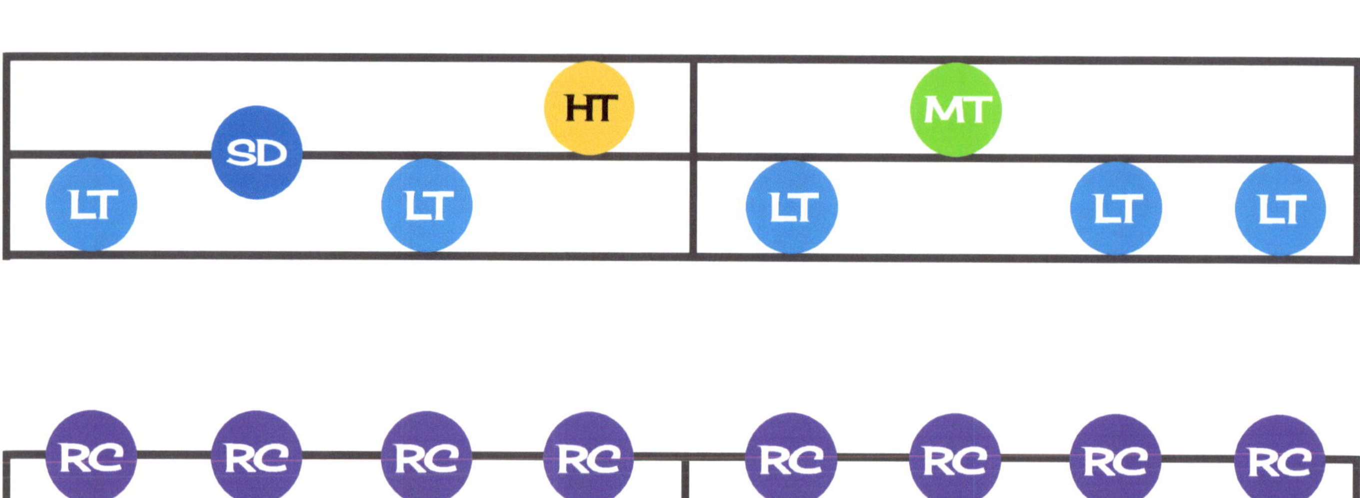

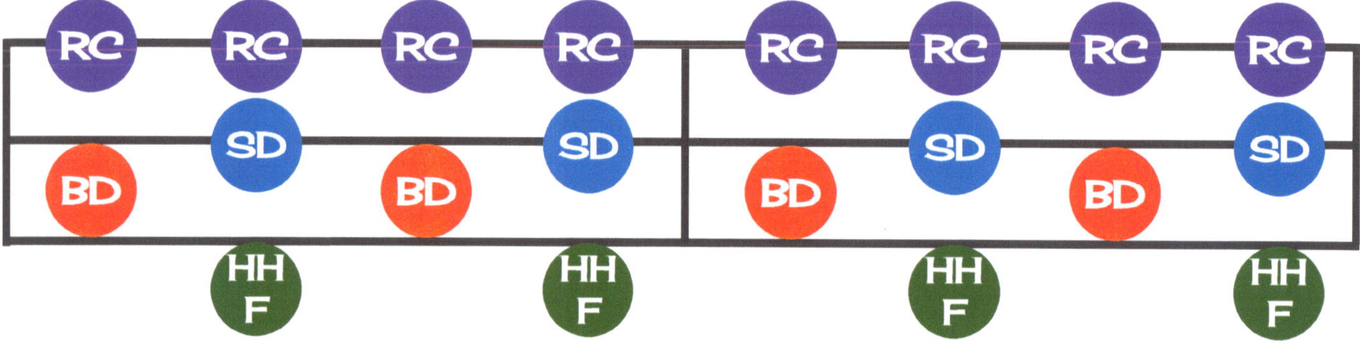

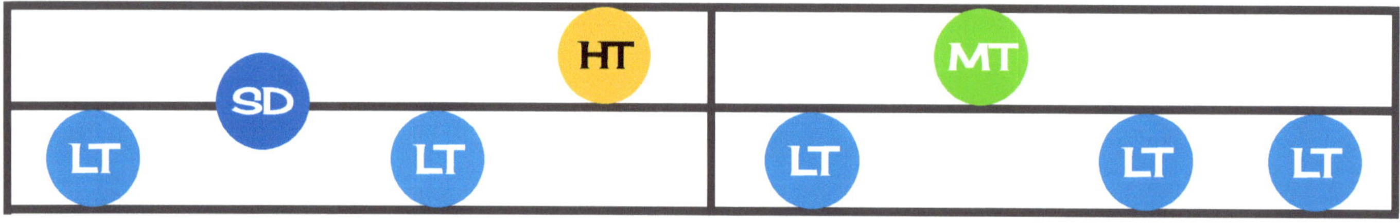

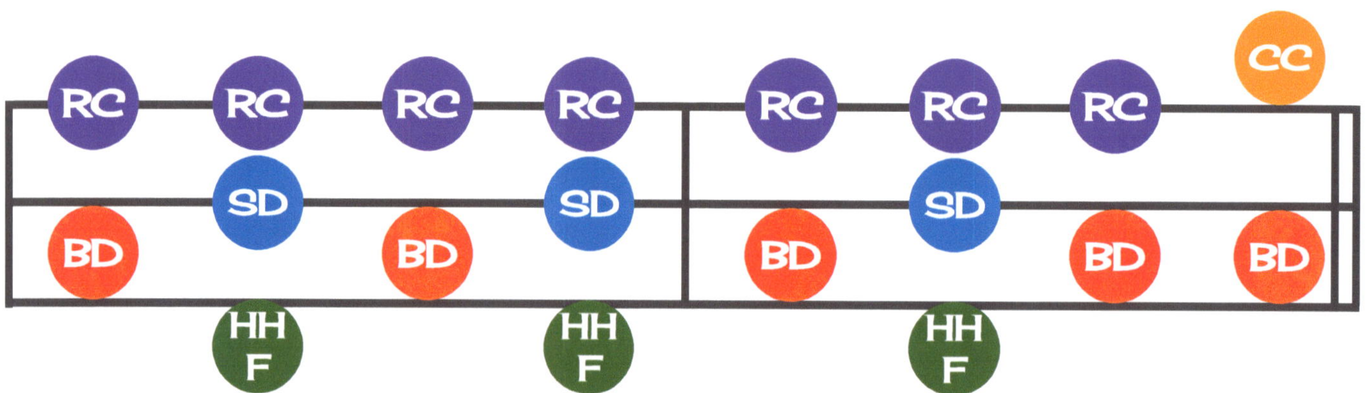

Drum Tools Word Search

Circle all the words you see in the word blank below.

All words are either side to side or up and down.

H	I	L	I	G	H	T	E	R	S
I	T	P	O	I	N	T	V	U	T
G	T	H	R	O	N	E	E	D	I
H	U	R	B	O	N	E	R	I	C
D	R	U	M	K	E	Y	Y	M	K
R	O	M	I	N	U	T	E	E	S
U	U	P	E	N	C	I	L	N	T
M	N	O	R	O	U	N	D	T	I
E	D	N	S	O	U	N	D	S	C
M	E	T	R	O	N	O	M	E	K

WORD BANK:

STICKS   THRONE   METRONOME

DRUM KEY   PENCIL HILIGHTERS

Drum Set Word Search

Circle all the words you see in the word blank below.

All words are either side to side or up and down.

A	B	C	D	H	I	H	A	T	S
B	A	S	S	D	R	U	M	N	A
C	S	O	C	K	U	M	A	A	H
D	S	C	O	H	O	O	L	R	I
M	E	C	R	A	S	H	L	I	G
I	V	A	S	E	S	L	S	D	H
D	E	L	O	W	T	O	M	E	T
T	N	I	B	O	R	A	O	M	O
O	S	N	A	R	E	D	R	U	M
M	S	N	A	K	E	Y	E	D	A

<u>WORD BANK:</u>

BASS DRUM   SNARE DRUM   HIGH TOM

MID TOM   LOW TOM   RIDE   HI-HATS   CRASH

Snare Drum Word Search

SNARE DRUM is hiding in this word search 5 times!

Each **SNARE DRUM** will either be up and down, or side to side.

Try and find them all!

S	S	N	A	R	E	D	R	U	M
S	N	A	R	E	D	R	U	M	S
S	A	R	E	N	D	R	U	M	N
N	R	D	D	E	R	O	M	O	A
A	E	R	R	D	U	L	L	M	R
R	D	U	U	M	M	O	M	S	E
E	R	M	M	S	N	A	O	U	D
D	U	S	S	R	E	D	O	M	R
R	M	N	E	D	R	U	M	S	U
U	S	N	A	R	E	D	R	U	M

Bass Drum Word Search

BASS DRUM is hiding in this word search 6 times!

Each **BASS DRUM** will either be up and down, or side to side.

Try and find them all!

B	A	S	S	D	R	U	M	U	R
A	B	A	S	S	D	R	U	M	U
S	A	S	S	S	D	R	U	M	B
S	S	S	S	S	R	D	B	B	A
D	S	Y	U	M	U	R	A	A	S
R	D	R	M	M	M	U	S	S	S
U	R	U	B	M	M	M	S	S	D
M	U	M	D	R	U	B	D	D	R
S	M	B	A	S	S	D	R	U	U
A	B	B	A	S	S	D	R	U	M

Drums Word Search

DRUMS is hiding in this word search 8 times!

Each **DRUMS** will either be up and down, or side to side. Try and find them all!

D	R	A	G	O	D	R	U	M	S
D	R	U	M	S	R	O	U	N	T
O	R	A	N	G	U	T	A	N	A
A	R	O	U	N	M	R	U	M	R
S	D	R	U	M	S	A	N	D	S
T	R	E	A	T	T	H	U	N	D
I	U	C	D	R	U	M	S	I	R
C	M	O	R	A	N	A	R	O	U
K	S	L	A	C	E	G	L	O	M
S	T	A	G	E	D	R	U	M	S

Cymbals Word Search

CYMBALS is hiding in this word search 8 times!

Each **CYMBALS** will either be up and down, or side to side. Try and find them all!

C	Y	M	B	A	L	S	E	C	C
A	C	Y	M	B	A	L	S	Y	A
P	Y	Y	L	A	B	S	T	M	P
C	Y	M	B	A	L	S	I	B	C
Y	M	O	O	L	C	B	C	A	Y
M	A	T	U	S	Y	A	K	L	M
B	L	C	Y	M	B	A	L	S	B
A	L	I	M	O	V	A	A	F	A
L	S	T	B	V	O	A	K	A	L
S	Y	Y	C	Y	M	B	A	L	S

Color the Drum Set

Choose your own colors and color in this drum set! Make it rock!

TITLE: _______________________

TITLE: _______________________

Composing Challenge 1

Write a solo using only Bass Drum and Snare Drum!

Composing Challenge 2

Write a solo only using the tom drums!

Composing Challenge 3

Write a solo only using the following instruments:

BD SD RC HH CC

Composing Challenge 4

Write a solo only using the cymbals!

Composing Challenge 5

Write a solo only using the following instruments:

Cut & Compose

With help from an adult, cut along the dotted lines, and you have your own cards to help you compose your own solos!

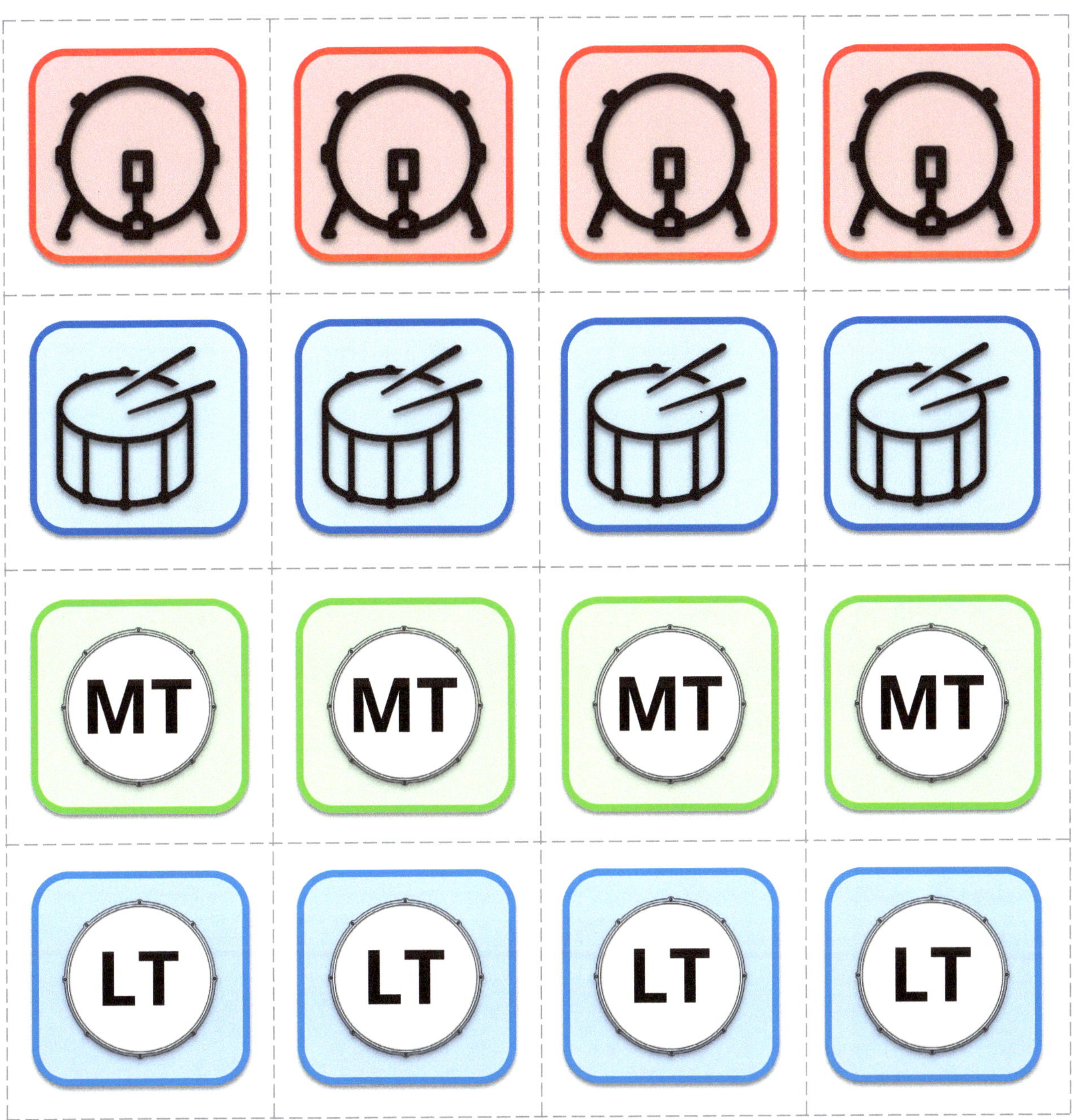

Cut & Compose

With help from an adult, cut along the dotted lines, and you have your own cards to help you compose your own solos!

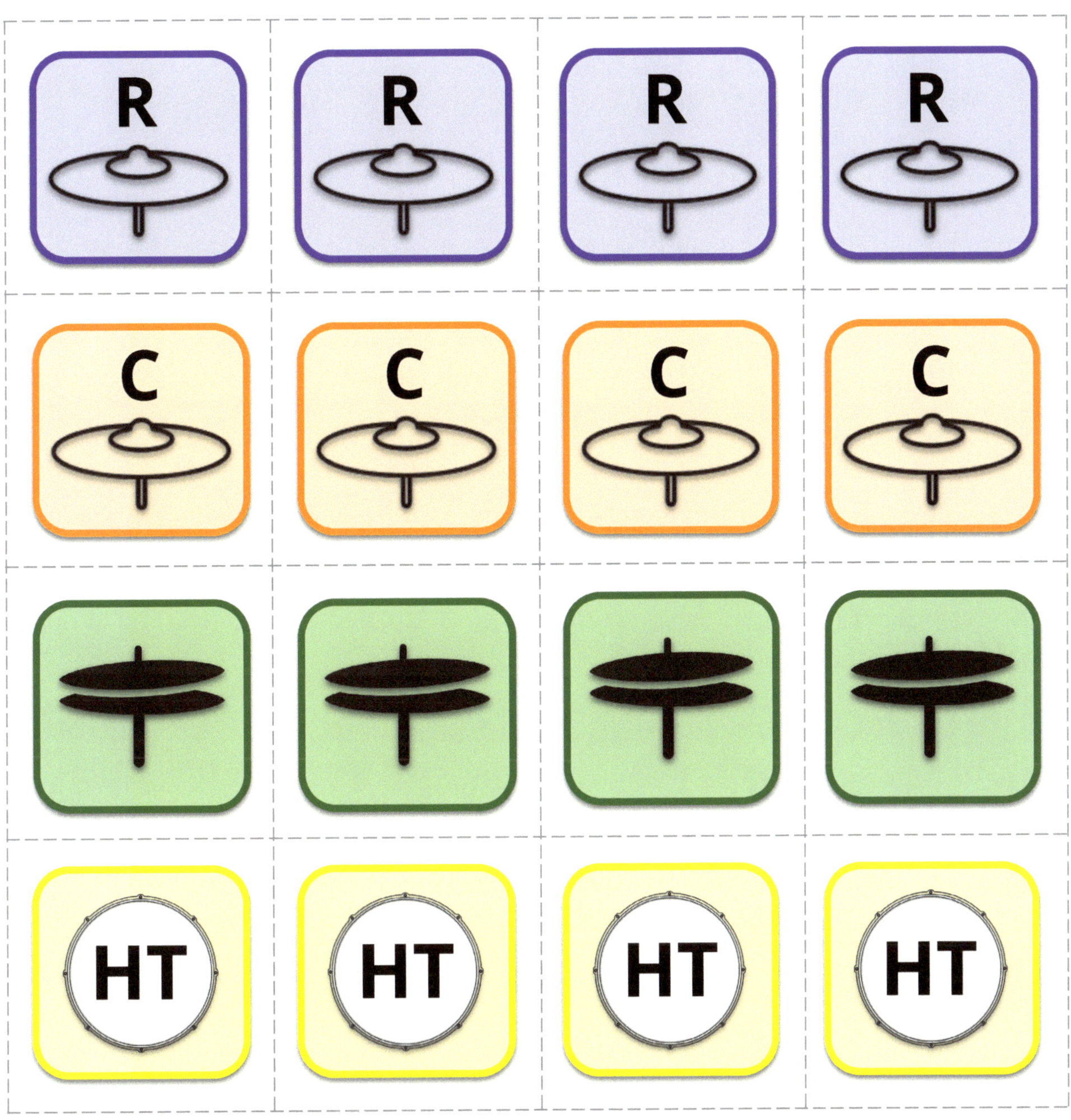

Cut & Compose

With help from an adult, cut along the dotted lines, and you have your own cards to help you compose your own solos!

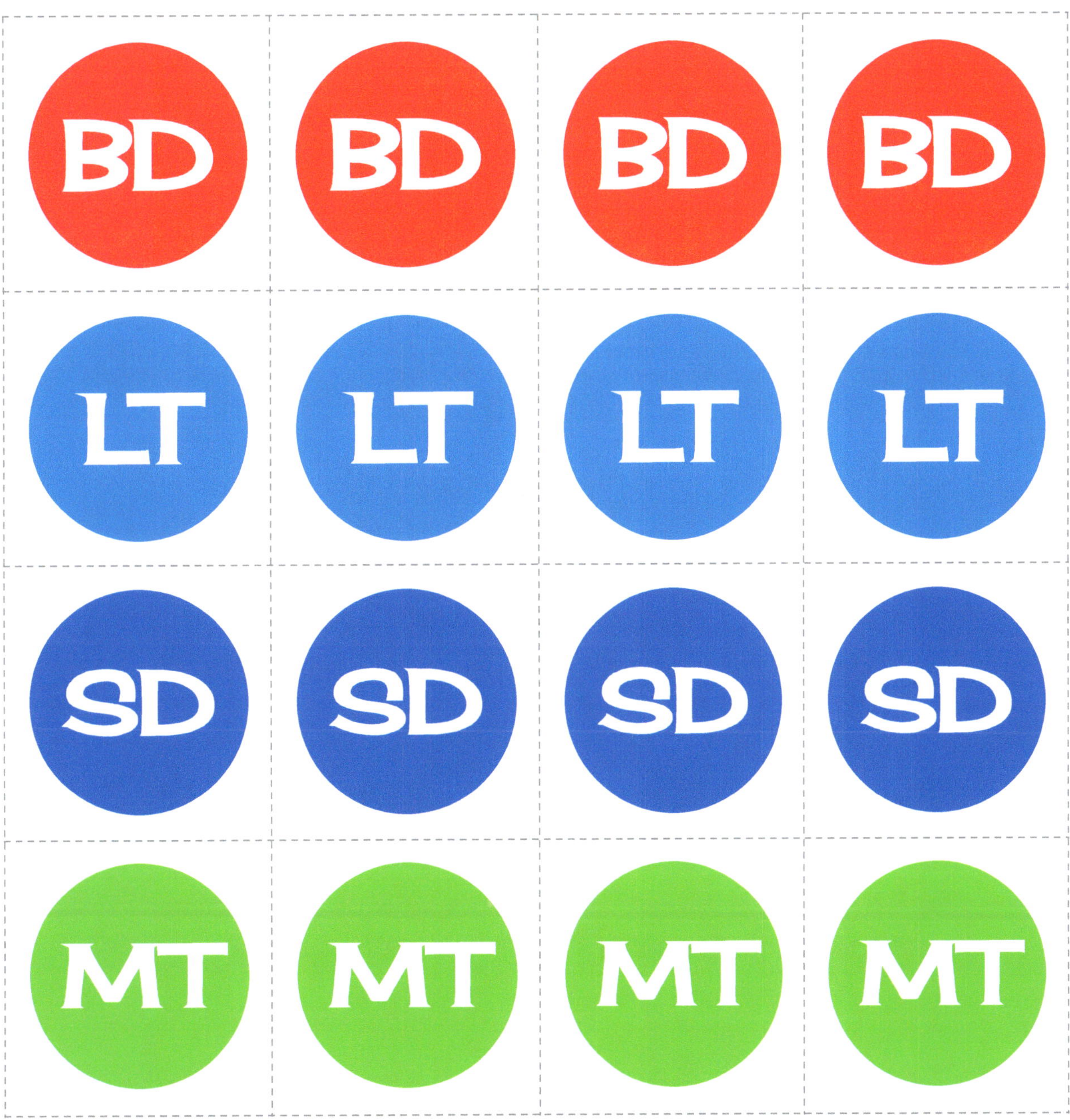

Cut & Compose

With help from an adult, cut along the dotted lines, and you have your own cards to help you compose your own solos!

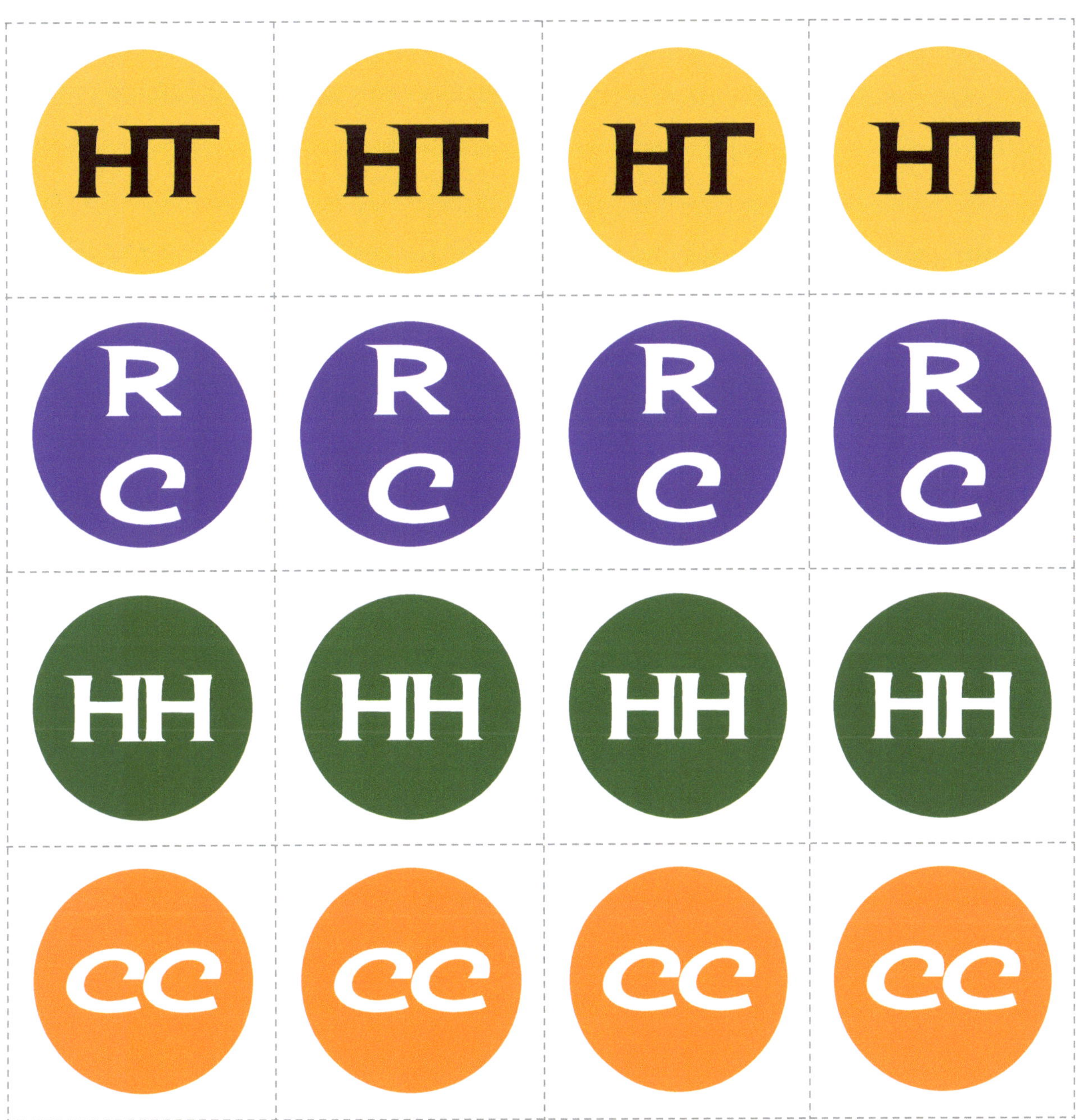